W9-DEZ-892

The Bedford Guide for Writing Tutors

Second Edition

Leigh Ryan
University of Maryland

BEDFORD BOOKS   BOSTON

Copyright © 1998 by Bedford Books
A Division of St. Martin's Press, Inc.

All rights reserved. No part of this book may be reproduced, stored in a retrieval system, or transmitted by any form or by any means, electronic, mechanical, photocopying, recording, or otherwise, except as may be expressly permitted by the applicable copyright statutes or in writing by the Publisher.
Manufactured in the United States of America.

2 1 0 9 8 7
f e d c b a

Editorial Offices: Bedford Books
75 Arlington Street, Boston, MA   02116

ISBN 0–312–16732–6

Preface for Writing Center Directors

In my years directing a writing center, I have longed for a single, short book that my tutors and I could learn from and that could serve as a resource for tutoring information and techniques. While I wasn't trying to make composition teachers out of engineering or psychology or dance majors, I did want the tutors to acquire some knowledge of the writing process and some strategies they could use as they worked with students. Because the book didn't exist, I gathered articles and excerpts from books and we read and discussed them, applying their points to our tutoring. I borrowed and invented assignments and exercises to help students learn and practice skills. And I tried to create an environment in which we could share our experiences and learn from one another.

Writing *The Bedford Guide for Writing Tutors* has given me the chance to create the short book I wanted. In it I discuss how tutoring fits into the writing process and offer tutors suggestions and strategies to help students improve their writing. I discuss specific kinds of students and assignments tutors are apt to encounter. I invite tutors to examine and consider their tutoring roles and remind them that they are professionals working with people. I even offer advice for those who are interested in taking on outside tutoring and editing jobs. I hope you will adapt this guide to your own needs and those of your writing center, spending more or less time on specific sections and supplementing with articles, handouts, and exercises you may already use.

All the exercises included in the guide directly connect with acquiring tutoring skills and strategies. Because many training programs require students to maintain a journal, I've included suggestions to help tutors get started with keeping a journal. My own preference is for a dialogue journal, a weekly exchange of friendly letters that I do with each tutor throughout training. As we share experiences, thoughts, and concerns, I allay fears and offer help, but I also learn much from my tutors about tutoring and writing. I have also included a typical tutor training assignment in which tutors investigate and discuss their own writing processes. Because some new tutors haven't been tutored before, I ask them to seek tutoring as they complete the assignment. Other exercises ask tutors to investigate how writing is taught at their school as well as to practice and discuss tutoring tools and strategies. I invite you to pick and choose, to rearrange, adapt, and tailor these exercises to your needs and those of your writing center. You might choose to do some before reading a chapter to get students thinking about issues and give them a reason to read more carefully.

Because tutors work with students, rather than just with papers, no complete texts of papers are included in this guide. I believe that looking at isolated papers to discuss how they might be improved can encourage tutors to correct papers in tutoring sessions rather than consider the needs and concerns of individual students.

I wish to express my thanks to those who reviewed an early draft of the guide: their suggestions and ideas helped greatly to clarify my thinking. They also continually reminded me that despite the variety of differences among writing centers, we share the same concerns.

Mary Jo Berger, Randolph-Macon College
Francis DeBernardo, University of Maryland
Jack Folsom, Montana State University
Diana Hacker, Prince George's Community College
Barbara Jensen, Modesto Junior College
Kate Mele, Roger Williams College
Julie Warmke-Robitaille, Santa Fe Community College
Molly Wingate, The Colorado College

A special note of thanks also goes to Colleen Ryan, Jack Aboud, Nelsa Nichols, and Matt Ryan, all of whom patiently listened, read, and advised.

Adding a chapter on computers and tutoring has reminded me anew of how diverse writing centers are. It has also reminded me of how important readers are to writers. For sharing their expertise and suggestions, I thank

Eric Crump, University of Missouri at Columbia
Donald Houch, University of Maryland University College
John Hyman, The American University
Debbie Kimberlin, University of Nebraska at Omaha
John Olson, Oregon State University
Becky Rickly, University of Michigan at Ann Arbor

At Bedford Books, my thanks again to Chuck Christensen, Joan Feinberg, and most especially Joanne Diaz for her cheerfulness and guidance. I am also grateful to Elizabeth Schaaf and Ara Salibian, who carefully oversaw the production of the book, and to India Koopman for her skillful copyediting.

Most especially, I wish to thank my former assistant directors, Rebecca Spracklen, Charles Magnetti, Francis DeBernardo, and Melinda Schwenk, and all the tutors who through the years have worked at the University of Maryland's Writing Center. I have learned so much from all of you.

Leigh Ryan

University of Maryland

Introduction for Tutors

If I could tell you one thing about tutoring, it's that your real task is to make changes in the way students go about writing. That may not be what you think about tutoring now, and it's certainly not what most students have in mind when they come to a writing center. Often, students' thoughts are something like the following: "Go in with writing assignment because I want a good grade. Tutor tells me where and how to fix what either of us identifies as problems. I fix problems and get a good grade."

Last summer, my writing center acquired the tutoring services of Annie, a bright graduate student who wrote well. To start her off, Annie and I met several times to discuss tutoring strategies, and I gave her information about the university's writing program as well as some articles to read. As I watched her tutor over the next weeks, however, I was often troubled. Annie seemed to want to do too much of students' work for them, and she often let sessions run over as she tried to cover the many problems she encountered in papers. She also seemed breathless, as if she wasn't really having much fun tutoring.

We talked frequently and at length, and I tried to help. We analyzed what she'd done in tutoring sessions. Finally one day, Annie blurted out, "It's just that I think every student should leave here with an A paper, or I'm not a good tutor. That's what's wrong. And I have to get over that." She was right.

It didn't happen immediately, but Annie finally came to recognize what her job as a writing tutor really involved: She was someone who could help writers sort through their ideas, clarify their thoughts, and then communicate them effectively to an audience. All of us, even those who write well, can use an ally like Annie when we write. Perhaps most important, she was also someone who could show students strategies for going about this messy task of writing more easily — for particular assignments and for all future writing.

How we go about tutoring — about doing what Annie finally understood as her real job — is the subject of this book. The eight chapters discuss the writing process and strategies for helping students with it. They offer practical advice for tutoring in general as well as for dealing with specific kinds of students and assignments.

The exercises give you opportunities to discover more about writing and tutoring and to practice what you've learned. Many of them work best in a class where tutors can share what they discover. If you are using this book on your own, you might want to respond to exercises in a journal.

My hope for *The Bedford Guide for Writing Tutors* is that it helps you to become an increasingly competent writing tutor. My hope for you is that, as you do so, you come to find tutoring as exciting and rewarding as I do.

Contents

CHAPTER 1

Being Professional

Tutoring students in writing can be an exciting, enjoyable, and rewarding experience. It is also a professional activity involving both responsibility and trust; therefore, tutors must observe certain principles of conduct in their relationships with students, teachers, and other tutors. Because you may begin tutoring at the same time that you start reading this book, you should be familiar with these principles at the outset.

As a tutor, you will help many friendly, hardworking, conscientious students become better writers. But you may occasionally encounter some difficult situations: One student may want you to do some of the work on a paper; another may want you to agree that a teacher has unreasonable expectations; still another may want you to predict a grade. The following principles will help you handle such situations.

1. *Teachers need to be sure they are evaluating a student's own work; therefore, never write any part of a student's paper.* Instead of writing sections of students' papers for them, use guiding questions and comments to help them recognize their difficulties and come up with their own solutions. Though you may sometimes recast a sentence or two as an example, be very careful about how much of the students' own work you revise. If you need more examples, make up some or find an exercise in a grammar handbook or guide to writing. If you find yourself tempted to revise too much of the students' work, put your pencil away.

2. *Never comment negatively to students about a teacher's teaching methods, assignments, personality, or grading policies.* As a tutor, you will hear students' comments about instructors, assignments, and grading policies. Recognize, however, that you cannot know what actually transpires in a classroom; even if you did, it is simply not professional to pass judgment. Keep in mind that students are relating their impressions or interpretations, and these may be incomplete or even inaccurate. More often than not, there are valid explanations for what may appear to be a problem. What seems to be an incomplete or imperfect description of

an assignment, for example, may be based on previous assignments or may have been elaborated on in class. If you truly cannot understand an assignment or grading policy, send the student back to the teacher.

3. *Never suggest a grade for a paper.* Some students may ask a question like "Do you think this paper's good enough for a B?" Other students may pressure you to suggest a grade, but assigning grades is the teacher's job, not the tutor's. Evaluating writing is a subjective matter, and your assessment may not be someone else's. Remember, too, that you cannot know all that has been discussed or explained in class, so you may have incomplete information about the assignment. Sometimes teachers outline criteria for papers on early assignment sheets. They may not repeat these criteria on later descriptions of assignments but may nonetheless hold students accountable for them. Even if a paper seems well written, it is wise to be judicious with your praise. A student may interpret your comment that this is a "good paper" to mean that it deserves an A.

   Suggesting a grade can only lead to trouble. A student's receiving a lower grade than you'd mentioned could create conflicts among the teacher, the student, and the writing center. A student who receives a higher grade than projected by a tutor might come to doubt the writing center's judgment.

4. *Never criticize the grade a teacher has given a paper.* Just as suggesting a grade for a paper can lead to trouble, so too can acknowledging to the student your disagreement with a grade. Sometimes a student unhappy about a grade will actively seek support for his or her dissatisfaction from a tutor. Even if you agree with the student, do not say so. Recognize that you may not be aware of all the factors that led to the grade. Students should first try to resolve concerns about grades with the teacher, and then, if necessary, talk with other appropriate people.

5. *Honor the confidentiality of the tutoring relationship.* Idle comments — whether praise or complaint — made about a student to others may get back to the student. Or the comments may be overheard by others who visit the writing center, making them wonder what will be said about them when they leave.

Being engaged in a professional activity has other implications for your behavior with students, and it also influences how you conduct yourself as part of a group, how you relate to other tutors, and how you function as a representative of the writing center to the rest of the campus. To make apprehensive students feel more comfortable, writing centers tend to deliberately project a cordial, inviting, relaxed atmosphere. Tutors reflect this ambience through their casual friendliness. Occasionally, however, they may be tempted to behave in too casual a manner, forgetting for the moment the professional nature of tutoring.

When students arrive, be pleasant and courteous. They may feel uneasy about showing their writing to a tutor, and those coming for the first time may be unsure about writing center procedures. Make sure everyone feels welcome. Although you may intend it as a gesture of goodwill, being flippant or sarcastic may put some students off.

Even if you are tired or under stress from school or job responsibilities, show a willingness to work with each student who comes in. Do not argue with other tutors about whose turn it is or throw a student up for grabs with a comment like "Who wants to work with this one?" Such behavior might well make a student wonder what kind of help a grudging tutor will deliver.

It is fine to be relaxed at the writing center, but excessively casual behavior — conducting intensely personal conversations, for instance — may offend students, especially those who come from different cultural backgrounds. You should also be considerate of other tutors. Delinquency or carelessness on your part might make someone else's job more difficult. Being professional means reporting for work on time or calling beforehand if something prevents you from being there as scheduled.

Tutors and students often work in close quarters, so be considerate and keep your voice down. If you have a few idle moments, take the initiative to see what you can do. Often small tasks like filing, typing, handling paperwork, or even watering plants need doing.

To the students you encounter, you represent the writing center. They judge the writing center not only by the competency of your tutoring but also by the attitudes, courtesy, and respect you display toward them and other tutors.

A journal provides a way to record your progress as a tutor, to give voice to your observations, and even to write your way toward solutions to problems you may encounter. The following exercise will help you get started.

EXERCISE 1A

Write in your journal at least once a week about your tutoring experiences — the successes, the problems, the questions — and your thoughts about them. Write about your observations regarding the writing process and working with particular kinds of students or assignments. Record your reactions to readings, writing assignments, or topics covered in tutor meetings or other classes involving writing.

You may keep this journal for your own use. Or you may do it as a dialogue journal (in effect, an exchange of friendly letters). Arrange for an audience — perhaps your director or another tutor — to respond to your writings on a regular basis. If you choose another tutor, respond to each other's entries each week. In this way, you can learn with and from each other. Record your thoughts in a notebook or on a computer disk and exchange those, or, if it is available, use e-mail. Do remember, however, to keep each other's writings confidential. Do not share them with others unless you secure permission first.

Because journal conversation is just that — conversation — students should feel free to use informal language.

CHAPTER 2

The Writing Process

As the writing center opens for another day, tutors exchange greetings, pour cups of coffee, and check their tutoring schedules for the first hour. Meanwhile, students check in at the reception desk. Then the tutoring sessions begin. . . .

As he takes a seat, Tom waves several sheets of paper. "Here are my notes," he tells the tutor. "I did a collecting project in my folklore class, and now I have to write a paper about what I learned from doing the project. I have a bunch of ideas, but I'm not sure which ones would be good to use."

Rummaging through her book bag, Maria pulls out a draft of an essay for a graduate school application. She describes it as "boring" and asks, "What can I do to make it more interesting for the people who read these essays?"

Louise thrusts her paper, a summary of an article on the role of psychology in education, into the tutor's hand. "I just want to make sure my paper is *right*," she explains. As she fishes another piece of paper out of her notebook, she adds, "We got this handout explaining summaries, and it's got a list of mistakes you can make in summaries. I know I didn't plagiarize, but I'm not sure about some of the others."

Marty puts his paper on the table and says, "I did this paper for my business writing class. I think the paper's okay, but I always have trouble with things like commas and semicolons. If you could just look at the punctuation . . ."

Mary takes a seat and gingerly proffers an assignment sheet to the tutor. "It's a paper for my history class," she explains shyly. "We're studying about the Revolutionary War, and we're supposed to pick a topic and research it. A ten-page paper seems so hard, and I don't really understand what to do."

Each of these writers is at a different stage in the writing process. Before we look at the specific stages, let's take a broader look at the writing process.

Years ago, teachers assumed that writing was a linear process whereby students simply took information already tucked away in their heads and put it on paper. They advised students to "write about what you know," make a formal outline of ideas, write the paper following that outline, and then revise, which usually meant checking for punctuation errors, misspellings, and other sentence-level problems. These teachers graded the final paper, encouraging students to take their comments to heart and apply them to the next paper, remembering, for example, to "give more detail" and write fewer "awkward" sentences.

But this model for writing did not seem to fit with what writers were actually experiencing when they wrote. A writer could start out to write a paper, say, on a visit to New York City, only to discover partway through that the paper really dealt with something else, like the different experiences he or she had with cabdrivers. And then there were the problems with outlines. Students were often told to write an outline before starting their papers and to submit the outlines with their final drafts. But if, as often happened, the content and focus of the paper changed as the student wrote, the outline no longer fit with the paper. The one for the New York City visit, for example, would have probably included details about hotels, restaurants, and sightseeing. Few of these details would have appeared in the final draft. In response to situations like this, many students simply wrote their outlines after writing the paper, not before.

To understand more clearly the weaknesses of this linear model of the writing process, look at the following list of writing experiences to see if you can identify with any of them. Have you ever

— written and rewritten for hours, only to find that you have two useful sentences from many pages?
— written a section midway through your paper that forced you to make significant changes in what you'd written in previous pages?
— carefully made a list of the important points to include in a paper and then discovered partway through writing that two of the points were unnecessary?
— struggled mightily to fit a sentence at the end of a paragraph and then discovered that it fit perfectly at the beginning?
— spent an evening writing and rewriting an introduction, unable to get it together, and then had the perfect introduction spring forth when you began writing the next day?
— tried to write a letter of complaint and found you had to write the angry, "no holds barred" letter before you could write the more controlled, reasonable one?

The work of composition researchers and theorists like Janet Emig, Sondra Perl, Linda Flower, Peter Elbow, and Donald Murray shows that the linear model of prewriting, writing, and revising is inadequate. We now recognize that writing is a process of discovery

— of exploring, testing, and refining ideas, and then figuring out the most effective way to communicate those ideas to a reader. As Peter Elbow explains, "Meaning is not what you start out with but what you end up with" (15). As writers, we continually return to earlier portions of a draft, generating new ideas and deleting others, writing and rewriting in order to move forward with the paper. Some writers make global revisions — major changes in content, focus, organization, point of view, or tone — after completing a first draft. Others follow the example of a student writer who recently explained to me, "As soon as I start writing even just a few words, I start revising." Throughout this backward and forward movement, we struggle to observe the constraints of writing conventions. Simultaneously, we go about the complicated tasks of making meaning and adapting the needs of the reader to our goals as a writer.

As you might guess from this discussion, we cannot outline the writing process as we can a recipe in a cookbook. No single set of simple steps can guarantee that we will produce an effective paper each time. As William Zinsser notes, "Writing is no respecter of blue prints — it's too subjective a process, too full of surprises" (63). Nonetheless, writing teachers and books on writing offer a variety of helpful descriptions of the process. These descriptions enable us to think of writing as something that happens in stages and to talk about it more easily among ourselves and to others. Most important, at each stage we can discuss a variety of workable strategies with the students seeking our help, strategies that fit with our goal as writing tutors: *to make the students we work with better writers by making changes in the way they produce writing.*

The following pages offer a general guide to the stages of the writing process. Each stage includes a brief discussion about one of the students introduced at the beginning of this chapter and how his or her writing concerns fit into that particular stage. In Chapter 4, you will find specific suggestions for helping with each stage of the writing process.

A General Guide to Stages of the Writing Process

PREWRITING

The prewriting stage consists of invention and planning. To generate ideas, we may use such strategies as freewriting, brainstorming, research, or observing. Then we must plan our writing, focusing our thoughts and ideas and considering how we should organize them. As an important part of prewriting, we also consider the audience we are addressing and our purpose for addressing them. Asking ourselves "To whom am I writing?" (audience) and "Why?" (purpose) helps us determine what information to include and how to present it. Then we can organize our ideas, at least loosely, into some workable plan.

Tom, who didn't know what to do with the notes from his folklore project, is at the prewriting stage. First, he needs to identify and assess his audience and his purpose. Then he needs to see how the information he has gathered fits with that purpose. Does he have enough information to at least start a draft? How can he effectively arrange the material he has?

WRITING

In the writing stage we get our ideas down on paper in an initial draft. Most people do their actual writing privately, but some students might find it helpful to draft a portion of a paper, like the introduction, in the writing center.

Consider again Tom's folklore paper. If his ideas for the paper are adequate, he might begin drafting the introduction and then discuss his work with the tutor.

REVISING AND EDITING

Revision consists of two stages: global revision, in which we improve the "big picture" of our papers (content, organization, tone), and sentence-level revision, in which we look at the finer points of our writing, strengthening and clarifying sentences. In the editing stage, we correct errors in grammar, punctuation, and mechanics.

Global revision. When making global revisions, we think big, asking questions like "Will my audience be able to follow and understand what I've written?" "How do I come across to my audience?" or "Have I included enough information?" In answering these questions, we often realize that major changes in content, focus, organization, point of view, and tone are necessary. Some students resist this stage, bringing their first draft of a paper to the writing center with the belief that it is their last.

Maria, the graduate school applicant, needs help making global revisions. She has a draft but wants to make it more interesting to the reader. To do that, she needs to first consider her audience and purpose for writing. Why is she writing to them and what will they be looking for? She can then consider what kinds of changes to make in her essay and perhaps rearrange, add, or delete sections to make her writing more effective.

With her summary of an article on the role of psychology in education, Louise, too, is most likely at the revising stage. Her teacher's list of "Properties of a Poorly Written Summary" includes being verbose or incomplete, plagiarizing, adding useless material, and being too subjective. As she and the tutor read through her paper, they will be able to determine what she may need to revise.

Sentence-level revision and editing. When making sentence-level revisions, we try to improve individual sentences by cutting excessive words, clarifying confusing or improperly constructed sentences, or trying to find more exact words for the ideas we want to express. In the editing stage, we correct errors in grammar, punctuation, and mechanics. (After revising and editing, we proofread, looking for typographical errors, omitted words, and other mistakes that we might have missed earlier.)

Remember Marty, who asked his tutor to help him check the punctuation in the paper for his business writing class? He needs help with the editing stage. (As you go over Marty's work with him, you may notice that he also needs to make sentence-level revisions.)

And what about Mary? If you recall, she seemed confused about how to begin her history paper and overwhelmed by the idea of producing ten pages. To help her get started, you might find it helpful and reassuring to talk about all the stages of the writing process. As she begins to see writing her paper as a series of smaller, manageable tasks, she might feel less overwhelmed.

The following exercises allow you to explore the writing process in several different ways: by considering how others describe the stages, by looking at how writing is taught at your school, by examining the language people use to talk about writing, and by taking a close look at your own writing process. You may do the exercises independently or in conjunction with a training course, and they can provide good starting points for group discussion.

EXERCISE 2A

Choose four different guides or handbooks on writing. Make a list of the terms they use to describe the stages of the writing process, and compare and contrast the ways they describe the stages. Set up the comparisons in the way that works best for you. You may want to sketch out an informal chart.

EXERCISE 2B

How are writing and the writing process taught at your school? To answer this question, you should explore a variety of resources. The following list offers suggestions for questions to answer and ways to go about this task. You may wish to do this exercise in small groups, working together or dividing up the tasks.

1. *Courses.* What writing courses are offered? Are there courses for basic writers? For English as a second language (ESL) students? For students not quite ready to take a regular composition course? Are there classes in intermediate or advanced composition? courses in business or technical writing or other specialized areas? Are some courses sequential?

2. *Course descriptions.* Are there written descriptions of these courses? Often school catalogs include short descriptions, but some writing programs offer more expanded explanations of the purpose and goals for each course. How does one course differ from another?

3. *Textbooks.* What textbooks (guides to writing, handbooks, readers, style manuals) are being used at your school? Your writing center or writing program office may have copies that you can examine. Or you might check the shelves in the school bookstore. Look through these texts. How are they organized?

4. *Syllabi.* Check to see if your writing center or writing program office has a file of sample syllabi. If not, you might find several teachers and ask them for copies. Does each writing course have a standard syllabus, or do teachers write their own? What kinds of assignments are included? Do they follow a particular sequence? How do instructors incorporate textbook material into their courses?

5. *Assignments.* How are assignments given? Are they taken from the textbooks? Do teachers provide assignment sheets explaining the assignments? To answer these questions, you might poll several instructors. Or you might check to see if there is a file of typical assignments in the writing center.

6. *Computers.* Is word processing a part of writing classes? How is it included? Do some or all classes meet in a computer lab? You might want to talk with a couple of instructors about how they use the computer lab for their courses. Personnel at the computer lab may also be able to give you an idea of how — and how widely — writing classes use the lab.

7. *Competency exams.* Do any of the writing courses at your school use competency exams? Are they given during the course or at the end? What format(s) do they follow? What aspects of writing do they stress? If your writing center does not have a file of competency tests used at your school, try to get copies of old tests or practice tests from instructors. You may also want to talk to instructors about how and why they use them.

8. *Writing-intensive courses.* Are there writing-intensive courses, perhaps as part of a writing-across-the-curriculum program? What defines these classes as writing intensive? Are there guidelines for these classes? What are they like? What, if any, writing textbooks (perhaps a handbook or style manual) do they use?

EXERCISE 2C

When students meet with tutors, they use a variety of terms to discuss their writing. Many students echo their teachers and the ways that writing is discussed in their classes.

The following is a list of common writing terms that you should be familiar with. Define the ones that you already know, and then use the textbooks and other resources used in your school's writing program or writing center to define the rest.

Audience:
Brainstorming:
Coherence:
Comma splices:
Composing process:
Emphasis:
Final draft:
First draft:
Format:
Freewriting:
Heuristics:
Invention:
Mechanics:
Organization:
Point of view:
Subject/verb agreement:
Thesis:
Tone:
Topic sentence:
Voice:

EXERCISE 2D

The preceding list of terms is by no means exhaustive, for we commonly use many other terms as we discuss writing with one another. Make a list of additional terms (with definitions) that might be used to discuss writing in your writing center. Your school may base its writing instruction on a particular textbook or approach to teaching writing, and you will need to be familiar with terms particular to that book or approach. Tutors at the University of Maryland Writing Center, for example, would add several terms from classical rhetoric, like *ethos, logos,* and *pathos,* because many writing teachers at this school use these terms in their classes.

To work with writers, you will need to become familiar with a variety of writing strategies. One way to begin is to start where you are an expert: with your own writing process. Because you have been writing for many years, by now you have some ideas about what works (and does not work) for you when you confront a writing task. But you have probably never taken a formal look at what you actually do from the moment you are given an assignment to the moment you hand it in. The following exercise asks you to write a paper in which you reflect upon your writing process.

© 1990 Tribune Media Services, Inc. Reprinted by permission.

EXERCISE 2E

How I write. When you are confronted with a writing task, how do you approach it? Do you spend days fretting about it? Immediately jot down ideas and then start playing with them? Think for days and then produce a first draft at one sitting?

And how do you go about actually producing a draft? Do you carefully assemble specific materials — like three sharp pencils and a legal size pad? Don comfortable clothes — perhaps a favorite sweatshirt — and sit down at the computer? Create an introduction that "will suffice" and then rework the introduction later? Write, pace the floor a bit, write again, pace again?

Do you write with the advice of a particular person — maybe a former teacher — echoing as you compose?

© 1982 Tribune Media Services, Inc. Reprinted by permission.

When do you begin to consciously consider your audience? From the outset? As you revise your first draft?

Do you seek the advice of others as you write? Do you read or show people drafts or parts of drafts? What kinds of feedback do you look for? When others give you suggestions, how do you factor them in?

How do you feel when you've completed the paper? Are you simply glad it is done? Are you convinced that one more pass would produce a better paper?

We all go about writing in idiosyncratic ways. We find what works for us and what does not; then we try to capitalize on the former and minimize the latter. Your task in this paper is to examine and discuss your own writing process, using the preceding questions as a guide. You may describe how you go about writing in general, or you may focus on a piece of writing that you have completed recently. Use other tutors as your audience. As you write, keep in mind that writing should delight as well as instruct.

This paper should be three to five pages long, and you should go to writing center tutors for assistance at least twice as you work on it. You may go at any point in your writing process, but work with two different tutors.

This assignment is an ideal departure point for group discussion. If possible, meet with a group of tutors and read your papers aloud to one another. Compare and contrast the different ways you each go about approaching a writing task. You will probably find that you have a variety of approaches. As others speak, take notes, first because you may pick up some hints for making your own process more efficient, and second to begin thinking about the kinds of suggestions you might offer to students who seek your help.

When you have finished discussing your writing processes, shift your attention to the two tutoring sessions you each had. One of the best ways to discover how people feel about an experience is to put yourself in their shoes. You are learning to be a tutor, but you have just had the experience of sitting in the other chair—that of the student being tutored—twice. Take five minutes to jot down your responses to the following questions and then discuss your answers.

— How did you feel about getting help from a tutor?
— What did the tutor do or suggest that you found helpful, both in terms of completing your assignment and in making you feel more comfortable about getting help with your writing?
— Conversely, what, if anything, did the tutor do or say that confused you or made you feel uncomfortable?

CHAPTER 3

Inside the Tutoring Session

Getting Started

It's not by accident that many writing centers appear welcome and friendly. To make writers feel more comfortable, centers are often furnished with plants, bright posters, easy chairs, and sometimes tables instead of desks. You too should try to put writers at ease. A casual but interested greeting and a smile can immediately make them less apprehensive about the prospect of sharing their writing with someone else. Be alert for those reluctant students who hover about the doorway, unsure about what to do. You might invite them in with a cheerful "Can I help you?"

A good way to begin a tutoring session is to introduce yourself. Ask the writer his or her name. Then, once you have found a comfortable place for the two of you to work, ask about the assignment and how it is going. If you have worked with the writer before, ask how the last assignment went. The exchange of pleasantries at the beginning of a tutoring session helps to establish rapport and gets the session off to a good start.

The best arrangement for tutoring is sitting side by side at a table. Such a setup suggests that you are an ally, not an authoritarian figure who dispenses advice from behind a desk. Sitting side by side allows you and the writer to look at the work in progress together, but you can still position your chairs to look at one another as you converse. If you do use a desk, have the writer sit at the side of it rather than across from you.

Keep the paper in front of the student as much as possible. If you are working at a computer, let the writer sit in front of it and let him or her control the keyboard. This placement reinforces the idea that the paper is the student's work, not yours.

Keep scrap paper and pencils handy, as well as a handbook and dictionary. Though it is generally a good idea to let the writer do most of the writing, you may wish to occasionally demonstrate a point in writing, or it may be more expedient for you to occasionally make notes for the writer.

Setting the Agenda

During the first few minutes, you and the writer will be setting at least a tentative agenda for the tutoring session. To do this, you first need to know exactly what the assignment is, including constraints such as length or use of outside sources. The simplest way to get this information is to ask the writer to explain what the instructor expects and then request clarification of any aspects that seem unclear to you. If the writer has an assignment sheet, read through it briefly to make sure he or she has not forgotten or misunderstood details, but not so quickly that you miss important information. Rather than discussing the assignment first, some tutors prefer to read through the assignment sheet, but some writers might feel uncomfortable waiting in silence for the session to continue. In addition, asking writers to articulate the assignment often allows you to uncover any misunderstandings they may have, especially as you become more familiar with typical assignments.

Once you know what a writer is working on, ask what you can do to help. In some cases, the writer will tell you exactly what kind of help he or she needs—for example, "the introduction just doesn't seem to say what I want it to" or "the paper reads too much like a list." Or the writer might identify a grammatical point, like subject-verb agreement or semicolon usage, that frequently gives him or her problems.

As you and the writer talk during these first few minutes, look for information that will help you understand his or her concerns and determine what you can do. Be aware that some writers will simply ask for help with "editing" or "proofreading," using these terms to cover any aspect of revising from major reorganization to eliminating wordiness or correcting comma splices. How you will spend your time depends on the following factors:

— where the writer is in the composing process
— the constraints imposed by the assignment itself, with the limitations inherent in it and those imposed by the teacher (length, number of resources, and so on)
— the time remaining before the paper is due
— the willingness of the writer to work with the tutor and improve the paper

Sometimes a writer lacks sufficient time to really benefit from the tutor's suggestions. There may be problems with the content or organization, for example, but the writer has time to correct only sentence-level errors. When you encounter such a situation, explain to the writer that you cannot deal with all aspects of the paper that may need attention but will focus on the most expedient ones.

Another important factor is the length of time allotted for each tutoring session. Once you have assessed the writer's needs, you will need to determine what you can realistically hope to accomplish in the time you have. Some writing centers schedule appointments for twenty or thirty minutes; others allow fifty minutes or an hour. Probably no tutoring session should last more than an hour. If it does, chances are that the writer will be overwhelmed by suggestions, or the tutor may end up doing too much work for the writer.

Three Effective, Powerful Tools

As a tutor, you have three powerful tools at your disposal: *active listening, facilitating* by responding as a reader, and *silence and wait time* to allow a writer time to think. Used in combination, they can help you to learn and better understand what writers' concerns or problems with writing may be. You can use them to induce writers to think more clearly and specifically about their audience, their purpose, their writing plan, or what they have already written. These tools also provide an excellent means of getting feedback to determine how well writers understand the suggestions or advice you have given them.

ACTIVE LISTENING

After exchanging pleasantries and settling down at a table, Sam and his tutor, Donna, begin their tutoring session. As you follow their conversation, pay particular attention to Donna's responses to Sam's comments and concerns.

> *Donna:* So, tell me what you're working on. What's your assignment, and what can I do to help?

> *Sam:* I'm taking this speech course on gender and communication. For our final paper, we're supposed to take five rituals connected with courtship and marriage — like the engagement ring, bachelor and bachelorette parties, the father giving away the bride, the white wedding dress — and analyze them. We're supposed to relate them to some of the concepts we've been discussing all semester. And it's due next Tuesday.

> *Donna:* That sounds like a really interesting assignment, like it would be fun to do. I haven't heard of that assignment before, so I'm a little confused. Do you have to do research for it? Tell me more.

> *Sam:* No. No research. Not really. Just what we've been doing in class. I don't know. Five to seven pages! I think it's kind of hard. I can think of rituals, but there are so many. How do I choose five that are good? I don't want to do the same ones everyone else is doing. By the time Dr. Timmons looks at my paper, he might be tired of reading about engagement rings and white wedding dresses. And then I don't know how to put them into some kind of order. I could

put the most significant one first, but then I'll end up probably trailing off into the least exciting one. Boring! And I have to have a coherent paper, so I need an introduction that kind of ties these five rituals together. How do I do that?

Donna: What I'm hearing you say is that this assignment is really frustrating you, and you just can't get started. It sounds like you're worrying about all of it at once. Let's see if we can get some kind of handle on this. Okay. You have to select five rituals.

Sam: Yes, like the ones I mentioned. But they're the obvious ones.

Donna: Perhaps. But I also heard you say that you're concerned about the length of your paper. Let's start with the rituals. You have to discuss five, but earlier you mentioned four of them—engagement rings, bachelor and bachelorette parties, wedding gowns, and fathers giving brides away.

Sam: Well, the *white* wedding gown. I know, but those are so obvious.

Donna: Are those rituals that you think you might have something to say about? Why did you choose those?

Sam: Yeah, you might be right. You don't think they're too common? Too obvious?

Donna: Maybe not. I can hear that you're very concerned that they're obvious, but if you have a lot to say about each, your paper could be really good. Probably better than if you picked something you might not know much about, like bridal shower games. Tell me more about the first one you mentioned. Let's see — the engagement ring.

When Sam talks about his assignment, he is clearly overwhelmed and frustrated. Rather than sorting the assignment out into workable tasks, he worries about content, length, engaging the reader, organization, and the due date simultaneously.

What Donna demonstrates in this scenario is *active listening,* a skill that takes energy and concentration. Instead of dismissing Sam's concerns, Donna grants them validity with statements like "What I'm hearing you say is . . . ," "It sounds like . . . ," "And I also heard you say that . . . ," and "I can hear that. . . ." She feeds back what she believes to be his message.

As the session continues, Donna *paraphrases* Sam's list of rituals, mirroring what she heard him say earlier. This paraphrasing accomplishes two purposes: It lets Sam know that she has heard and understood him, but it also serves as a way to check perceptions and correct any possible misunderstandings. For example, as Sam notes, it is not just the wedding gown that is important, but the fact that it is white.

Donna also uses *questions* to invite Sam to expand on or continue his thoughts. She asks, "Why did you choose those?" and urges him to elaborate by saying, "Tell me more about. . . ." Notice that

A Note about Asking Questions

Questions can help you learn more about a writer's attitudes and specific problems with writing or with particular assignments. Questions fall into two broad categories — open and closed.

An open question like "What have you been working on in class?" or "What can I do to help?" is broad in scope and requires more than a few words in response. Usually an open question begins with *What, Why, When,* or *How.* Responses to such questions, especially at the beginning of a tutoring session, can help you determine the writer's attitude toward the task at hand. Asking "What can I help you with?" invites more response than "I see you're working on a definition paper." A question like "How is the class going?" may help you learn more about the writer's performance as well as about his or her expectations.

A closed question is one like "Have you got a description of your assignment?" "When is your paper due?" or "Do you have some ideas for that section?" Such questions require a yes or no or a brief, limited response. Not only do such questions yield specific information, but the answer to a question like "Who is your teacher?" may tell you something about the class or assignment if you've dealt with other students who also have that instructor.

these questions are open ones. Rather than requiring decisive yes or no responses, they give Sam room to continue his thoughts and to develop them.

Finally, Donna uses *I statements* when she says "I'm a little confused" and "I can hear." This approach places the burden of understanding on her rather than on Sam. If she had said, "You're not explaining things clearly," Sam might well have become defensive. Because Donna's questions and comments are not antagonistic, Sam is more likely to seek out and remedy the causes for her confusion rather than justify his apprehensions.

What we can't see in this scenario is Donna's physical engagement in the conversation, her *body language.* An active listener generally communicates interest and concern by posture and eye contact. Donna is probably leaning slightly forward, her feet on the floor, and looking directly at Sam. Her gestures of friendliness and approval, like nodding or smiling in agreement, also help to assure him that she is interested and following what he is saying.

FACILITATING

Shelly comes to the writing center with her first draft of a paper for an Introduction to Poetry class. Reproduced here are the first two paragraphs.

Emily Dickinson, her poetry, and her style of writing all reflect her own feelings as well as her own ultimate dreams. Her withdrawal from the world and her impassioned art were also inspired in part I think by a tragic romance. A series of tormented and often frankly erotic letters were found to prove that this unsuccessful romance had a strong impact on her emotions — enough impact to seclude her from any outside life. This paper concerns two of Emily Dickinson's poems, number 288 and number 384, which are both prime examples that reflect the dejection she was experiencing.

In poem number 288, Dickinson reveals her loneliness. In line number one, she introduces herself as "Nobody," as if it is her plural name. Nobody also refers to someone that people do not know much about. I think the word Nobody uses both meanings in this poem. She then asks the reader if they are Nobody too.

Shelly's paragraphs probably raise many questions in your mind. Looking only at the first sentence, for example, you might wonder, What feelings are reflected? What dreams? And how does Dickinson's style reflect these? But such questions only reflect the confusion Shelly is experiencing at this stage in her writing. Though it is clear she has thought about some ideas, she remains unfocused. She needs help with sorting through, clarifying, and articulating those ideas.

The best way to assist Shelly is to focus on her thoughts and ideas rather than on the paper itself. Instead of making judgments about her draft, describe your reactions as a reader and ask questions that invite her to further examine, explore, and clarify her own ideas and approaches. By reacting as a reader you are *facilitating* (a word that means "making easier").

The following paragraphs discuss the functions that facilitative questions and comments may serve. They offer examples as well as suggestions for applying them to Shelly's paper.

Reacting as a reader. Comments like "I'm confused," "I get lost here," "From your introduction, I expected to read . . . ," and "This is what this sentence or paragraph means to me. . . . Do I have the right idea? Is that what you meant?" simply and honestly reflect your response to a paper as you read it. They invite writers to elaborate and, in so doing, to clarify ideas for you and for themselves.

➤ *What you might say to Shelly:* An introduction should tell the reader what the paper will be about, but Shelly's introduction mentions several aspects of Dickinson's poetry, and it is unclear which one(s) her paper will focus on. Reacting as a reader, you might explain, "In your introduction, you say that Dickinson's poetry reflects her feelings and dreams and her dejection about the unhappy romance that inspired it. But when I finish that paragraph, I'm confused. I'm not sure exactly what your paper's going to be about." The *I* statements place the burden for the confusion on you, not Shelly, and invite her to resolve it. She will perhaps struggle to articulate her intended focus, but in doing so she will probably come to some new realizations about that focus.

Requesting information. Questions such as "Can you tell me more about . . . ?" can help students clarify their thinking, consider the whole paper or an aspect of it more critically, refocus their thoughts, or continue a line of thinking further.

➤ *What you might say to Shelly:* Of the many poems Emily Dickinson wrote, Shelly chose two to discuss. Requests like "Why did you choose these two poems? Can you tell me more about them?" give her an opportunity to articulate and examine the reasons for her choice. Doing so should help her better understand what it is she wants to say about the poems.

Requesting clarification. When students' answers or writing are vague, encourage them to clarify points by asking, "What is your idea here?" "What are you thinking?" "What do you want to say?" "What do you want your reader to know in this paragraph?" "How does this idea connect with what you said before?" "What do you mean by . . . ?" or "Tell me more about. . . ."

To be sure you are following and understanding what a student intends, restate the content of the message: "What I'm hearing you say is. . . . Do I have it right?"

➤ *What you might say to Shelly:* Shelly's reference to *feelings* is vague. Ask her to clarify the term: "You say Dickinson's poetry reflects her feelings. What do you mean by *feelings*? Which feelings?" Such questions will lead Shelly to consider her intentions more carefully and come to a clearer understanding of what she means to say. As she responds, you could encourage her to relate her answers to the two poems, asking "How are Dickinson's feelings reflected in the two poems you chose?"

Developing critical awareness. Writers sometimes plan or write whole papers without adequately considering audience or purpose, and one of the best questions you can pose is "So what?" That question, or versions of it — such as "Why does anyone [your audience] want or need to know about that?" — forces writers to think about why they are addressing their audience. "So what?" also makes them consider and justify other points in the paper, as do questions like "Why would that be so?" and "Can you give me an example of . . . ?"

➤ *What you might say to Shelly:* Shelly has singled out the word *Nobody* as significant, but she does not clearly explain why. To encourage her to justify its importance, you might say, "You indicate that the word *Nobody* is important in this poem. Why would that be so?"

Refocusing. To get writers to refocus or rethink their writing, it is useful to get them to relate their approach to another idea or approach, using questions like "How would someone who disagrees respond to your argument?" "How is that related to . . . ?" or "If that's so, what would happen if . . . ?"

➤ *What you might say to Shelly:* Shelly's draft is not far enough along to begin refocusing her material. Let's suppose, however, that you know something about Shelly's topic, an aspect that she should at least consider in her thinking. You might ask, "Didn't Dickinson also have a phobia, a fear of public places? How might that relate to her 'withdrawal from the world'?" Note that your request does not demand that Shelly consider this aspect; it merely asks her to examine whether she should consider it.

Prompting. To get writers to continue or follow their line of thinking further, encourage them with questions like "What happens after that?" or "If that is so, *then* what happens?"

➤ *What you might say to Shelly:* As Shelly articulates her ideas about Dickinson's poetry reflecting "feelings," she will probably mention loneliness, because she includes that word in her draft. Encourage her to continue thinking along those lines with questions like "What words or phrases suggest to you that she was lonely?" and "How do those words or phrases show loneliness?"

As a facilitator, you function as a sounding board or mirror, reflecting to students what you hear them trying to communicate. Your stance is an objective one, for your purpose is to evoke and promote students' ideas, not to contribute your own. As you become increasingly comfortable with tutoring and better able to size up the students you work with, you may feel more comfortable with occasionally offering opinions or suggestions for content, but beware. The paper must remain the responsibility of the student.

SILENCE AND WAIT TIME

Try this experiment. Get a watch or clock with a second hand. At the start of a minute, turn around or place the clock out of sight. When you think that a minute has elapsed, look back. How close did you come? Thirty seconds? Forty-five? Chances are you stopped a little too soon, and that is what we tend to do when we try to make ourselves wait; we jump in a little too soon.

As a tutor, you should learn when and how to pause and be silent in a tutoring session. Occasionally, writers need time to digest what has been discussed or to formulate a question. They also need time to think about a response when you pose a question. Often tutors are tempted to quickly rephrase a question or even answer it themselves when a writer does not respond after a moment or two. If you feel this temptation, try waiting a little longer than you think you should and then wait some more. This deliberate use of wait time communicates to students that they are expected to think. You might even consider creating an excuse to get up and leave for a few minutes; go to the rest room or get a drink of water.

Thinking time is especially important when a new aspect of a topic arises, and writers may even need a few moments on their own to do some writing. Try initiating short breaks that allow students five or even ten minutes to freewrite, brainstorm, or draft a section of a paper. At other times, you might give them time to complete an activity that relates to what you have just been discussing. You might ask them to revise a portion of their draft or correct certain problems with grammar, mechanics, or punctuation. Or they might complete a short grammar exercise. When they finish, you can review their work with them.

The Many Hats Tutors Wear

© 1995 Creators Syndicate, Inc. Reprinted by permission.

A tutor's role varies from session to session. With one writer, you ask question after question to help him figure out what he has to say about a scene in *Beowulf.* With the next you explain the various ways of defining a term in a definition paper. In the midst of this session, the student vents some frustrations about being a returning student and balancing her time, so you direct her to a series of workshops for returning students. Then an ESL student appears. He just cannot get his subjects and verbs to agree, so you pull out a piece of paper and start explaining. In your tutoring, you function variously as an ally, a coach, a counselor, a commentator, a collaborator, and a writing "expert."

The Ally. You are a friend who offers support to a writer who is coping with a difficult task — writing a paper. You are sympathetic, empathic, encouraging, and, best of all, you are supportive and helpful. You explain things in terms the writer can understand. You answer questions that may seem silly or stupid, but you take them seriously. You understand. After all, didn't you just explain that you have a history paper due tomorrow and you do not expect to get much sleep tonight?

The Coach. In sports, coaches instruct players and direct team strategy. They do not actually do the work for the team, but rather they stand on the sidelines observing how the team functions, looking at what is going well and what needs improvement. Likewise, you stand on the sidelines. The work that writers do needs to be their own, but by asking questions, making comments, and functioning as a reader, you encourage writers to think through problems and find their own answers. You suggest ways of accomplishing the tasks. You explain how to organize a comparison and contrast paper, clarify the rules for using a semicolon, or explain strategies for invention and even help students to implement them.

The Commentator. Sports commentators give play-by-play accounts, but they also give a picture of the whole game as it progresses. Likewise, you describe process and progress in a broader context than a student might otherwise see. As Muriel Harris explains, "The tutor-commentator provides perspective, makes connections to larger issues, gives students a sense of when and how they are moving forward" ("Roles," 64). You enable writers to see a paper as a whole by working with them to establish goals and by explaining what work lies ahead. You help them acquire strategies and skills that will work not just for this paper but for others. You point out that making a correction in spelling or punctuation is not just a matter of following a convention but rather of making their writing more accessible for a reader.

The Collaborator. You know that students are supposed to do all the work themselves, but you are discussing ideas for a paper with a sharp student. She has read *The Awakening* and has focused on examining color imagery in it. You have just read the book, so you know what she is talking about. She mentions the dinner scene, and you have an idea about the color yellow in it. Do you keep it to yourself? Probably not. So the two of you exchange ideas about the imagery; she profits from your input, and you from hers.

If you share your ideas with students, however, you need to be wary of two potential problems. Writers should always be responsible for and in control of their own papers. Lazy or unsure writers may try to rely on you to produce most or all of the ideas for papers that should be their own — in effect, to write the paper for them. Conversely, the overzealous tutor may usurp papers, interjecting too many ideas and leaving writers no longer in control of the paper, confused, and perhaps less confident about their writing abilities.

The Writing "Expert." You may not be a writing teacher or a writing expert; nonetheless, students usually come to you assuming that you know more about writing than they do. The truth is, you probably do. Just by being a tutor you become more knowledgeable about writing. You are an example of the adage that we learn best when we explain something to someone else.

But what do you do at those times when you realize that you are in over your head, that you do not know how to explain a grammatical point or the options available when writing a résumé? The simple answer is to admit that you do not know and seek help. Check a textbook or ask another tutor, who can often be an excellent resource. Occasionally, you may need to turn the writer over to a more knowledgeable tutor. In that case, you might sit in and learn something for the next time you encounter a similar situation.

The Counselor. A student's life includes much more than the writing assignment at hand, and often other issues and concerns interfere with getting the assignment done. Sometimes, you may find yourself playing the role of counselor, listening to students' concerns and dealing with such issues as attitude and motivation. You may encounter a transfer student who is disgruntled because she has lost credits in changing schools, or a returning student who wonders if he can continue to juggle his job and school successfully, or a graduating senior who has lost interest in school and just can't seem to get motivated. In such cases, you offer support, sympathy, and suggestions as appropriate. You refer students to workshops or programs on campus: conversation groups for ESL students, time management or study skills seminars, résumé workshops, GRE reviews.

EXERCISE 3A

The roles described above are not the only roles tutors play. Sometimes you may find yourself functioning as a parent, therapist, actor, guru, or comedian. Exploring the many roles tutors might play can be interesting and informative. Make a list of all the roles you can imagine tutors playing, then list the strengths and weaknesses of each. How do these strengths and weaknesses affect tutoring? If you are working with other tutors, you might do this exercise in groups, with each group exploring the same or different roles.

When Is a Tutor Not a Tutor?

Once your friends and neighbors — or even students you work with — realize that you are a writing tutor, they may seek your help with assignments outside the writing center. Except in special cases that only you can decide (helping your roommate or a co-worker, for example), it is best to restrict your tutoring to the writing center. Otherwise you may find yourself coerced into spending your study or sleep time working on someone else's paper.

EXERCISE 3B

The following role-playing activities will help you practice active listening, facilitating, and using silence and wait time. If you are not using this book in conjunction with a class or training program, try to gather a group of tutors from your writing center who are willing to participate. Some of you will play a tutor or writer; others will observe the tutor's actions and words. (Role players might want to take a few minutes to jot down notes before beginning.) Following are descriptions of the responsibilities for each role.

Writer. Assume that you need to write a letter on one of the topics on page 26 and that you are seeking a tutor's help to explore your ideas and begin arranging them effectively. You will need to anticipate readers' objections to the ideas you express in the letter. Use your imagination to come up with convincing arguments and objections. (Note that you do not have to *write* the letter. You are in the preliminary stages of writing.)

Tutor. The writer is seeking your help with writing a letter. Your task is to help the writer

1. explore persuasive arguments;
2. explore the audience's potential objections to those arguments and potential rebuttals to the objections; and
3. begin planning an effective organization for the letter.

At the same time, you must

4. keep all your ideas to yourself and make *no* contributions to the content or organization of the letter; and
5. pass *no* judgment on any of the ideas the writer suggests. Instead, ask questions that help the writer focus and clarify ideas. (Remember to practice active listening, facilitating, and using silence and wait time.)

Observer(s). As the "tutor" works with the "writer," look for examples of active listening, facilitative language, and silence or wait time. Make brief notes as you observe examples. (Your notes need not include a sentence's content, only enough to indicate that the tutor is being facilitative: "I can hear . . . ," "What do you think . . . ?," and so on.

You might want to try different letter topics, trading roles as you move to a new topic. Each participant would thus get a chance to be a tutor, a writer, and an observer. After each session, group members should talk about how it felt to play the different roles. Observers should also share their impressions. What strategies did tutors use and how effective were they? How could tutoring sessions have been improved?

Letter topics

1. Spring semester is nearly over, and your parents have been looking forward to having you at home for the summer. But you wish to live and work away from home, perhaps at the beach or near your school. Select the place where you want to live for the summer and write a letter to your parents explaining your reasons; try to convince them that your living away from home is a good idea.

2. A number of students who use the writing center have indicated a wish for additional writing center hours. Write a letter to the director either supporting or opposing extended hours.

3. As the parent of a preschool child, you find that attending school poses some difficulties. Write a letter to the president of your school requesting that the school start a day care facility for students' children. (If your school already has a day care facility, ask that its hours be extended or assume that it is in danger of being closed and ask that it remain open.)

4. Write a letter to the president of your school asking for a change from giving grades for courses to using a pass-fail approach (or the opposite, if your school already offers pass-fail courses).

5. You are determined to participate in an exercise program while you are home for the summer, but you know you would be more apt to stick with it if you have company. Write a letter to your friend, who will also be home then, advocating a particular exercise program (such as swimming, weight training, or aerobics) and asking him or her to join you.

6. You have an opportunity to attend a three-day conference for writing tutors, but one of your professors frowns on people missing class. Write a letter to that professor explaining and justifying your request.

7. You and some friends have decided to go somewhere for spring break. Write a letter to persuade your friends that all of you should spend your time swimming in Cancun rather than skiing in Colorado. (Substitute other places and activities if you wish.)

8. Write a letter to the president of your school suggesting that a specific campus program be started or continued. (Some suggestions: an orientation course for new students, a writing center, a math center, a study abroad program, a particular internship.)

9. Your parents do not think it is a good idea for you to have a car on campus, but increasingly you wish to have one. Write a letter to your parents explaining your reasons.

10. Your younger brother or sister is considering buying a computer but is not sure how useful it would be. Write a letter explaining why a computer is (or is not) a good investment for him or her.

CHAPTER 4

Helping Writers throughout the Writing Process

Like the writing process, tutoring is dynamic. The interaction between tutor and writer, as questions, answers, and ideas flow back and forth, largely determines the content and direction of a tutoring session.

This chapter provides some guidelines and strategies for working with writers at particular stages in the writing process. What works with one writer, however, may not be as successful with another; therefore, you need to be ready with a variety of approaches and to be flexible about using them. As you become more proficient at tutoring, you will develop your own style and be able to add your own suggestions to those given here.

Prewriting

CONDITION:	Student is unsure about where or how to begin.
ACTIVITIES:	Discuss.
	Brainstorm.
	Freewrite.
	Collect/list/select.
TUTOR:	Questions.
	Reflects or mirrors.
	Suggests.
	Supports.

FINDING AND EXPLORING A TOPIC

Tutors can help writers discover what it is they want to say by using a variety of techniques. Brainstorming (or listing), freewriting, and clustering are discussed here, but you may want to check writing handbooks and textbooks to learn about others.

Brainstorming, or listing. Brainstorming involves focusing on a topic and tossing out, thinking through, and refining ideas to find ways to approach the topic. As writers list and play with ideas on a particular topic, ask questions to prod and encourage them to think more and reach further.

In response to the "How I Write" assignment in Chapter 2, Andrea came up with the following list of ideas:

wear comfortable clothes
get my desk completely clear
keep rereading the assignment sheet
PROCRASTINATE
write out some ideas on paper, put them on my computer, and
   move them around
call my dad and read the paper to him
write — rewrite — rewrite — rewrite
make sure I have a strong (funny if possible) introduction
put my hair in a ponytail
try not to use a form of "to be" in the first sentence
recall Ms. Coakley — my English teacher sophomore year

Following is Andrea's list reproduced again. The questions in parentheses are suggested questions a tutor might ask to prompt her to think and generate more ideas.

wear comfortable clothes (*Such as? Why?*)

get my desk completely clear (*Why?*)

keep rereading the assignment sheet (*When? To get started? As you write? Why? How does reading it over and over help* you?)

PROCRASTINATE (*Why did you put this word in caps? How do you procrastinate? What do you do? Why do you procrastinate?*)

write out some ideas on paper, put them on my computer, and move them around (*What do you mean by "move them around"? What do you do after that? Do you work only on the computer after that?*)

call my dad and read the paper to him (*Why? How does that help?*)

write — rewrite — rewrite — rewrite (*What do you mean by "write"? Why did you write "rewrite" three times?*)

make sure I have a strong (*funny if possible*) introduction (*Why? How do you do that?*)

put my hair in a ponytail (*Why? How does this relate to wearing "comfortable clothes"?*)

try not to use a form of "to be" in the first sentence (*Why? How does this relate to having "a strong introduction"?*)

Ms. Coakley — my English teacher sophomore year (*How did she affect your writing? What is there about what you learned from her that affects your writing today?*)

As writers' ideas evolve, paraphrase or mirror what you have heard them saying to clarify, check, and sum up lines of thought. Pose questions that guide them toward considering the audience, such as "What does your audience know about . . . ?" or "How can you make that clear to your audience?"

You might also play devil's advocate and suggest an opposing viewpoint to writers. Responding to you will force them to examine their own ideas more thoroughly.

Freewriting. Ask writers to put pen to paper (or fingers to keyboard) and simply let ideas on the topic flow for ten minutes. Tell them to write words, phrases, sentences, or questions but to ignore punctuation and spelling. If they get stuck, tell them to rewrite the last few words over and over until the juices begin to flow again. For writers working on computers, it can be helpful to darken the screen so they don't get caught up in reviewing what they've written.

The following paragraph was written by Rick, responding to the topic of tarot cards.

> What do I know about tarot cards? You can tell your fortune with them. How accurate are they? I had this lady read mine at the Renaissance Festival last month. She was pretty accurate. I'm not sure how many there are. How do you learn to read them? Did anyone ever do any scientific investigation of them? Results? Where did they come from/start? Tarot cards. Tarot cards. The word "tarot" sounds funny, sort of foreign. Do people all over the world use them? Sometimes in crossword puzzles — the word. What's on the cards? Pictures. Of what?

When writers are finished, review what they have written with them, looking for key words, phrases, or questions that seem promising. Focus on those and discuss or brainstorm.

Rick's paragraph offers a wealth of details to explore further. The tutor might ask questions that will help Rick uncover more possibilities in key words and phrases like *accurate, learn to read them, foreign* [word], and *scientific investigation.* Rick's reference to having tarot cards read at the Renaissance Festival might lead to questions about where one goes to have tarot cards read.

Clustering, or branching. With the writer, make a diagram with the central topic in the middle. Then, as you talk with the writer about aspects of the topic, ask how these aspects relate to the central topic and draw branches that show the relationships. (This technique not only helps writers explore their subject but also suggests how they might organize their ideas.)

The following diagram shows how one writer explored the topic of wetlands with a tutor. They began with the central topic — wetlands — in the middle. As they discussed aspects of the topic, the tutor asked questions about why and how each aspect related to the central

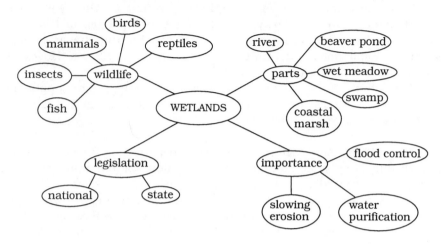

topic. Eventually the writer ended up with four issues related to wetlands: parts, wildlife, importance, and legislation — each of which had several subissues.

Other suggestions. With most writers, asking probing questions and discussing the answers can be enough to help them explore and generate ideas about a topic. For those who find coming up with ideas more difficult, finding a different perspective or way of looking at a topic can be useful. Asking writers to engage in one of the following exercises won't generate a paper, but, at the least, it will give you and them some avenues to investigate:

1. Imagine a scene that relates to the topic and describe it. Try the same thing with a sound or smell.
2. Imagine yourself as someone else — your older brother, your mother, your boss. How would that person look at the topic? What would he or she say about it?
3. Write about the topic in a letter to someone you feel comfortable with.
4. If you could write this paper without constraints, what would you write about and how would you go about it?

PLANNING TO WRITE

Once writers have generated sufficient ideas to get started, you can help them organize those ideas and plan to write. A note of caution: Some writers want to begin organizing a paper when they have only a few sketchy ideas, but continuing down this trail usually leads to a weak paper. You can help writers avoid this pitfall by helping them make sure they have clearly identified their audience, their goal or purpose in relation to that audience, and what they hope to accomplish in the paper. There are several ways you can help writers to plan and organize:

1. Ask if they know the conventions of and formats for the kind of paper they are working on. What does a cover letter accompanying a résumé typically include? What are the options for organizing a comparison and contrast paper or a definition paper? What should be included in a lab report? If students are unsure, explain. If you, too, are unsure, check a handbook or guide to writing.

2. Help writers explore options by mapping out how the paper might be organized. Rather than making a formal outline, which can be too rigid and confining for many writers, suggest that the writer generate a more informal kind of diagram such as a list or flow chart similar to the following. Writers can easily see the general shape of the paper but will feel freer to shuffle parts if necessary.

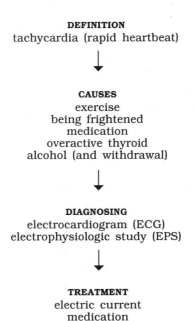

DEFINITION
tachycardia (rapid heartbeat)
↓

CAUSES
exercise
being frightened
medication
overactive thyroid
alcohol (and withdrawal)
↓

DIAGNOSING
electrocardiogram (ECG)
electrophysiologic study (EPS)
↓

TREATMENT
electric current
medication

EXERCISE 4A

There are many strategies to use in prewriting. Check a handbook or writing textbook to learn about other techniques. Then choose one and explain it to other tutors, showing how they might use it in tutoring. If time allows, demonstrate the technique.

Writing, Revising, and Editing

© 1996 United Feature Syndicate, Inc. Reprinted by permission.

MAKING GLOBAL REVISIONS

CONDITIONS: Writer has a draft.
              Writer has time to revise.

ACTIVITIES: Find out where the writer feels the
              draft needs improvement.
              Point out where the draft needs improvement.
              Explore possibilities.

TUTOR: Questions.
              Reflects or mirrors.
              Offers suggestions and opinions.

When helping a writer make global revisions, consider his or her paper's development and organization.

DEVELOPMENT
Did the writer
— follow through on points
  raised in the thesis?
— find enough supporting
  details and examples?
— explain relationships
  between ideas?

ORGANIZATION
Did the writer
— organize according
  to a particular scheme or
  format? or
— organize according to the
  needs of a specific audience?

By first talking with the writer about his or her paper's audience, topic, content, and structure, you get useful information and also give the writer the opportunity to indicate troublesome areas. As you then read through the paper together, you can compare what he or she has told you with what is actually on the page.

One of you should read the paper aloud. Asking writers to read can engage them more in the tutoring session, but explain that you will interrupt whenever you have a question or comment. Occasionally, you may prefer to read, reacting and commenting as you go. In any case, don't simply let writers sit there and watch you read silently, for any discomfort they may feel will only increase.

As writers talk about their ideas or read aloud, ask questions or comments to help them clarify their thinking and offer suggestions for improvement. At this stage, focus on the larger issues of content and organization. Not only are they more important than matters of style or mechanics, but you might otherwise end up spending much of the tutoring session on a section that is ultimately deleted.

Some suggestions:

1. Read the paper as a naive reader, and indicate those places where it needs more specific details. For example, if you read a sentence like "Watching the university's production of *Hamlet* was an exciting experience," ask what the writer means by "exciting." What exactly was it about this production that made seeing it exciting? If you read something like "My grandfather was a kind and generous person," ask for some specific examples or anecdotes that show the grandfather's kindness and generosity.
2. Stop at the end of a paragraph or section of the paper to summarize what you have just read and explain what you anticipate will follow. If what you say does not match the writer's intended message, he or she can see where misinformation, extraneous details, or other cues misdirect the reader.
3. Don't overwhelm the writer with too many suggestions for improvement at one time. Instead, single out one or two concerns and work on them. Sometimes it is better to select problems that are fairly easy to deal with to give the writer a more successful tutoring session. You can indicate that other areas need work and suggest that the student make another appointment to attend to them.

MAKING SENTENCE-LEVEL REVISIONS

CONDITIONS: Writer has a satisfactory draft.
Writer has time and motivation to revise.

ACTIVITIES: Read carefully, preferably aloud.
Consider each paragraph, sentence, and word.

TUTOR: Helps in reading.
Points out *kinds* of problems.
Questions.
Mirrors and reflects.
Offers opinions and suggestions.
Demonstrates techniques for improvement.

Sentence-level revisions involve strengthening and varying sentences as well as refining style. Inappropriate or imprecise language, wordiness, and choppiness are common problems in student papers. To help writers recognize these problems and learn to correct them, concentrate on a small section — a paragraph or several sentences. Later, writers can apply what they have learned to the rest of the paper. This approach also reminds writers that they are ultimately responsible for revising their papers.

Some suggestions:

1. To improve the voice of the paper, ask the writer, "Do you talk like this?" Discuss the use of language in the paper and then help the writer rework a small section and eliminate, for example, stuffiness or stilted words and phrases.
2. To eliminate wordiness, go through several sentences word by word with the writer to determine if each word is really necessary. You might also read wordy sentences back to the writer and then read the sentences again, leaving out what you think are excess words. Ask the writer to consider whether the words you have omitted are necessary.
3. To improve choppy writing, have the writer read the paper aloud. (Often, it is easier for the writer to detect choppiness when reading aloud than when reading silently.) You might want to have the writer revise some problem sentences in the tutoring session.
4. If the writer tends to use several prepositional phrases in a row, read a few sentences aloud. As you read, accent the choppy effect such phrases produce and then show the writer how to eliminate at least some of the phrases. Changing "running in the morning on the track on the campus keeps one fit" to "A morning run on the campus track keeps one fit" makes the sentence less choppy and less wordy yet retains the meaning.
5. Ask the writer to check his or her work for overuse of *be* verb forms. He or she can improve emphasis by replacing these forms with more vigorous verbs and eliminating passive voice constructions. If you notice that the writer overuses *be* forms and the passive voice, ask him or her to circle all the verbs in a passage and to then look at them and tell you what he or she notices.

EDITING FOR GRAMMAR, PUNCTUATION, AND MECHANICS

CONDITIONS:	Writer has a satisfactory draft.
	Writer has time and motivation to make corrections.
ACTIVITIES:	Read carefully, perhaps aloud.
	Consider each sentence and word.
TUTOR:	Helps in reading.
	Points out *kinds* of errors.
	Questions.
	Mirrors and reflects.
	Demonstrates techniques for correction.

Often, tutors worry that they must be thoroughly familiar with grammar rules, but that is not true. Good readers usually recognize a problem, though they may not always be able to explain it technically. If you are unsure about a rule or term, check a handbook. Guides to grammar, punctuation, and mechanics are called handbooks because they are intended to be conveniently carried for ready reference. Another handy and excellent reference that should not be overlooked is another tutor.

When you encounter problems with grammar, punctuation, or mechanics, paint a larger picture for writers. Explain that such errors distract readers from the paper's content. If readers pause to notice misplaced commas or misspellings, they lose the thread of the paper for a moment and must reorient themselves to continue reading. In the process, the paper's content becomes less compelling.

As you discuss grammatical points, be flexible with your vocabulary. What one writer knows as a "fused" sentence, another calls a "run-on." In addition, writers may be unfamiliar with terms like "comma splice" or "independent clause."

Muriel Harris wisely suggests turning the process of understanding over to writers by offering enough explanation to start them off and then inviting them to "find and revise all instances of whatever problem was discussed, asking questions as they proceed; to reformulate the principle for themselves in terms they are comfortable with; to write their own sentences demonstrating the rule; to cite uses of the rule in their own papers if that seems helpful; or to explain how the rule works in their sentences" (*Teaching* 120).

Serious problems with grammar, punctuation, and mechanics frequently permeate student papers. Concentrate on a small section — a paragraph or several sentences — to help students recognize and learn to correct these errors. Later, students can go through the rest of the paper and apply what they have learned.

Some suggestions:

1. Have writers read their papers aloud. In doing so, they often make corrections as they go, for the ear frequently judges more accurately than the eye. In addition, their changes afford you the opportunity to encourage them by pointing out that they really do know how to recognize and correct some of their errors.
2. Point to an error and ask a general question, such as "Do you see a problem here?" You might underline several sentences that reflect the same problem and ask the writer to read them aloud. If the writer cannot see the problem, focus on a single sentence. If he or she still remains unclear, explain the error and see if he or she can identify it elsewhere.
3. Ask writers which sentences they feel uncomfortable with and then ask why.

© 1987 United Feature Syndicate, Inc. Reprinted by permission.

EXERCISE 4B

Individually or in small groups, develop a handout that you and other tutors might use with students. The handout may offer help with a stage of the writing process, discussing, for example, prewriting techniques, or it may explain and offer an exercise for a grammatical point.

As you work, keep your audience firmly in mind. Make sure that your explanations are clear and complete and that your vocabulary is appropriate for the students you work with. Do not make the mistake of one tutor, a sports buff. In an effort to generate interest, he developed an exercise using sports jargon; students unfamiliar with some terms found the exercise confusing.

EXERCISE 4C

Working with handbooks and other writing center references. When you are tutoring, questions will come up that you cannot answer on your own. You may be uncertain about the parts of a proposal, a rule for using semicolons, or documentation according to the American Psychological Association (APA) format. In these cases, you will sometimes have to check references as you help writers. Such resources vary from writing center to writing center, but most centers have a collection of writing guides and handbooks as well as a file of explanations and exercises.

To familiarize yourself with the resources available in your writing center, explore them and try to note at least two places where you could find the following information.

1. accepted formats for business letters
2. an explanation and exercise on subject-verb agreement
3. the definition of a dangling modifier, with examples
4. strategies for tightening wordy sentences
5. rules for when to spell out numbers or use figures
6. exercises for correcting comma splices
7. advice on writing and formatting résumés
8. a discussion of subordination for emphasis
9. an explanation of cause and effect as a pattern of development

10. the format for documenting a selection in an anthology using the Modern Language Association (MLA) style
11. the rules for use of *who* and *whom*
12. ways to avoid using sexist language
13. an explanation of passive and active voice
14. the conventions for referring to authors in the text of a literary paper
15. a list of logical fallacies with explanations and examples

CHAPTER 5

The Writers You Tutor

The writers you tutor will have varied backgrounds, competencies, learning styles, and attitudes that affect their thinking and behavior. Some writers — those with writing anxiety, basic writing skills, or learning disabilities, or those for whom English is a second language — may present special challenges for tutors. Knowing specific approaches or strategies for tutoring these writers makes sessions with them more beneficial. In addition, many of the strategies and approaches can be useful in tutoring all students.

It is also worthwhile to remind ourselves that learning style and cultural background, as well as happenings in daily life, affect the ways each of us handles a writing assignment. Some of these influences you may never know about (a student's concerns about family or financial problems, for example). But it is important to be aware that they can be present. As you work with students, your words and actions should convey sensitivity and understanding; each student deserves to be treated fairly and with respect.

The Writer with Writing Anxiety

Calvin and **Hobbes**   by Bill Watterson

© 1995 Watterson. Distributed by Universal Press Syndicate.
Reprinted by permission.

As an undergraduate, I attended classes with Kathy, who panicked the moment she heard the words "write a paper." Rather than take notes as the teacher gave instructions, she thought only about the monumental task of producing a paper and tuned out the details. As we left class, Kathy would ask me, "What are we supposed to do? How long is it? When is it due?" Kathy had writing anxiety.

Writing anxiety can take many forms. One student frets because he can't simply put pen to paper (or fingers to keyboard) and immediately produce a good piece of writing. Another student dislikes writing so much that she puts off getting down to work and finds herself approaching the deadline with little behind her but worry and procrastination. Still another student writes and writes and writes, trying to get what he has to say "right."

Though the specific suggestions you offer each of these students may vary, it is always helpful to present yourself as a sympathetic ally. When Joan first came to me, she described herself as "desperate." "Why can't I just sit down and write?" she asked. "Isn't that what everyone else does?" As we discussed her concerns, I shared my own frustrations about writing, and she began to see that she was not alone. We worked together on her next few papers. Like most of us, Joan struggled to get her ideas down on paper, but she wrote well. Eventually she decided that helping others with their writing would also help her, and she became one of my best tutors.

Likewise, you might tell students about some of your writing frustrations. Acknowledge that writing is indeed hard work, not only for them, but for everyone. Just telling students that experienced writers often find it difficult to sit down and apply themselves to a piece of writing can be surprisingly reassuring. But you should also tell them that the satisfaction of producing a well-written paper is enormously rewarding.

You might try one or more of the following strategies when working with a student who has writing anxiety.

1. Briefly explain the writing process. Point out that beginning as soon as possible and allowing plenty of time actually makes the task easier. Getting words on paper helps students figure out what they want to say. Starting early also allows time for the unconscious mind to play with the ideas they have consciously gathered.

2. Help students break the assignment into a sequence of specific, manageable tasks. Then help them set up a reasonable schedule with deadlines for completing the various parts. This planning will also enable students to make use of the writing center during the writing process and can prevent small problems from becoming big ones.

3. Point out that breaking down the process of writing a paper into specific, manageable tasks can help writers feel degrees of success along the way. Rather than planning to sit down for an evening to "write the paper," a student might set out to draft an introduction and work out a tentative organization for the rest of

the paper or plan to revise a particular section of the paper. Approaching tasks this way enables students to leave their desks several hours later with a sense of having accomplished what they set out to do, rather than with disappointment or frustration that the paper isn't done yet.

4. Suggest that students make firm writing appointments with themselves and build in rewards. They can promise to work for a set period of time, with a reward at the end — a favorite television show, a telephone call, a bowl of ice cream, or some other treat. The rewards may sound silly, but the strategy often works.

5. Remind students that a rough draft is exactly that — rough. Especially in the early stages, writing needs to be free-flowing rather than perfect. Students should be concerned with getting ideas on paper and not get bogged down with finding the "right" word or making each sentence perfect before beginning the next one.

The Writer with Basic Writing Skills

In *Errors and Expectations*, Mina Shaughnessy perceptively illuminates the difficulties that students with basic writing skills have in producing effective academic writing. In this landmark book, Shaughnessy describes these students' problems with handwriting, punctuation, syntax, grammar, and spelling and then discusses the difficulties caused by their lack of familiarity with the concepts and forms of academic writing. Throughout this book and in her other publications about basic writing, Shaughnessy addresses the issue of the teacher's attitude. Repeatedly, she underscores the importance of respecting students' intelligence, making the point that basic writing students are not stupid but rather uninformed or misinformed. Further, she points out that basic writers do not necessarily apply grammatical rules incorrectly but rather use a different set of rules, acquired from speaking nonstandard English. Likewise, their writing reflects a lack of familiarity with the conventions for showing relationships among parts of a piece of writing rather than ignorance of the relationships themselves. As Shaughnessy explains:

> For the BW [basic writing] student, academic writing is a trap, not a way of saying something to someone. The spoken language, looping back and forth between speakers, offering chances for groping and backing up and even hiding, leaving room for the language of hands and faces, of pitch and pauses, is generous and inviting. Next to this rich orchestration, writing is but a line that moves haltingly across the page, exposing as it goes all that the writer doesn't know, then passing into the hands of a stranger who reads it with a lawyer's eyes, searching for flaws. (7)

Following are several general suggestions for working with basic writers. If you will be tutoring such students frequently, probably the best way to prepare is to read *Errors and Expectations*. In addition, you might look at other books and articles on basic writing.

1. Take care to be supportive, respectful, patient, and encouraging. Students with basic writing skills often feel especially frustrated and even defeated by the task of writing.

2. Talk with students about their perceptions of writing and of the writing process. Help them to understand that the writing process moves from the messy beginnings of conceiving and tentatively ordering ideas to getting those ideas on paper and making meaning of them, first for the writer and then for the reader. By discussing the larger process, you reassure students that they do not have to produce perfectly formed ideas and writing from the start. When you explain the editing stage, emphasize that this stage ensures that errors will not distract readers.

3. Help students develop and convey meaning by explaining what you think they said in a sentence or passage. For example, after reading a concluding paragraph, you might say, "Your last paragraph says that you've shown four ways students can reduce stress, but I only remember three: [list them]. Did I miss one? Can you show me where it is?" By responding to students this way, you can help them see where the meaning of their writing does not match their intentions.

4. Have students read their papers aloud or, better yet, into a tape recorder. Listening to themselves can help students identify weaknesses in development, coherence, and sentence structure. This activity also reinforces and encourages students' ability to recognize their own weaknesses.

5. Look at punctuation not in isolation but as a part of communicating ideas effectively. If a student struggles to combine two sentences, use that example to talk about the appropriate punctuation rather than simply handing the student an exercise on commas or semicolons.

6. Do not overwhelm students with too much information or too many suggestions at one time. It is better to cover one or two areas well so that students can master them and feel successful. You can attack other problems in later sessions.

The Writer for Whom English Is a Second Language

English as a second language (ESL) writers can sometimes pose a challenge for tutors. Their cultural backgrounds include different ways of looking at the world, different attitudes and ways of thinking, and different notions of what constitutes acceptable writing or appropriate student behavior. Sometimes they are serious students who do well in most classes and are unaccustomed to encountering difficulties with a course; therefore, they find their problems with writing in English especially frustrating. Becoming proficient in a second language is a slow process, and ESL writers' difficulties involve not only language but also unfamiliar customs and ways of thinking.

To get an idea of what some ESL writers face as they attempt to acquire a second language, look at the translation of an English sentence in the box.

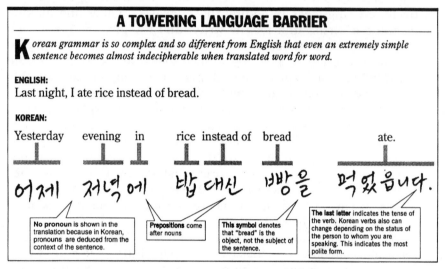

A TOWERING LANGUAGE BARRIER

Korean grammar is so complex and so different from English that even an extremely simple sentence becomes almost indecipherable when translated word for word.

ENGLISH:
Last night, I ate rice instead of bread.

KOREAN:

Yesterday evening in rice instead of bread ate.

어제 저녁 에 밥 대신 빵을 먹었습니다.

No pronoun is shown in the translation because in Korean, pronouns are deduced from the context of the sentence.

Prepositions come after nouns

This symbol denotes that "bread" is the object, not the subject of the sentence.

The last letter indicates the tense of the verb. Korean verbs also can change depending on the status of the person to whom you are speaking. This indicates the most polite form.

© 1992 *The Washington Post.* Reprinted with permission.

As with any student, respond first to the content and organization of ESL students' papers. Fixing sentences that may later be discarded is a waste of time. Find out what the assignment is and determine if the paper fulfills the purpose. Listen to what students are trying to say on paper and help them make sense of it.

Encourage students to talk through what they want to say in each paragraph — in other words, to briefly describe each paragraph's focus and content. This nonevaluative approach is especially helpful with students who are unaccustomed to questioning authority (and to them, you are the authority in the tutoring situation). As you work with students and their papers, ask questions that will help you understand what they are trying to communicate. Paraphrase what they have said to see if you have understood correctly.

No one can absorb a great deal of information at one time. In fact, too much help can be overwhelming and can make students feel even less secure about writing. It is wiser to concentrate on one or two problems at a time so that students can understand them and feel some degree of success. You can point out other problems, but leave them for subsequent tutoring sessions.

English can sometimes be illogical, and learning it can be difficult. As you work with students, strike an appropriate balance be-

Cultural Differences

Culture is defined as the beliefs, customs, and behavior patterns that distinguish a particular group of people and make up the background and experience of individuals within that group. How people think about themselves and others; behave with family, friends, and strangers; choose and prepare food; dress for different occasions; and celebrate holidays are determined by their culture.

When you tutor someone from a similar background to yours, you will both think and behave in similar ways; however, differences, especially in the areas of interpersonal and written communication, may become apparent when you tutor someone from a different culture or subculture. For example, in some cultures, questioning authority is frowned upon, and you may find students who are reluctant to ask you questions or admit they don't understand something. The amount of personal space people desire differs among cultures, and you may tutor students who make you feel uncomfortably crowded as you work together. Whatever differences you encounter, it is important to treat each student with respect and sensitivity.

Likewise, acceptable ways of presenting information differ among cultures. Americans tend to value the direct approach, but some cultures believe that meaning should be implied rather than spelled out directly. Still others approach a problem by giving its detailed history first, information that we might find unnecessary. We need to recognize such differences as cultural and explain appropriate rhetorical patterns in English.

Enumerating all the differences among students from different cultures and subcultures is impossible and even undesirable. Such a list would be incomplete at best, and it also runs the risk of stereotyping. Though you want to be aware of differences, you should not assume, for example, that every student you meet from a particular culture embodies what you know about that culture. What is important is that when you encounter cultural differences, you respect them for what they represent — different ways of looking at the world.

tween sympathy and encouragement. Even as you show understanding of their problems, reinforce what they do know and encourage them to learn and apply rules.

Following are some suggestions for working with ESL students.

1. Take pains to put students at ease. In some cultures, asking questions is impolite, so encourage students to ask questions if what you have said is confusing or unclear.
2. Give directions plainly. Watch students' expressions and ask questions to see if they comprehend your explanations. If you are not sure whether a student understands something you have said, ask him or her to explain what you have said or to give you

an example. Often ESL students may be too embarrassed to admit they are unsure. They may smile and nod in agreement but still be confused. Be patient and, if necessary, explain again.

3. If a student does not understand a comment or explanation, rephrase it. Do not raise your voice or simply repeat the same words.

4. If you have difficulty understanding an ESL student, watch for facial expressions as he or she speaks. The combination of watching and hearing can help you follow what the student is saying.

5. Many ESL students write better than they speak. Do not assume that because you have trouble understanding a student's speech, he or she will have significant problems in writing.

6. Generally, students should do most, or even all, of the writing in tutoring sessions; however, with some ESL students, handling all the tasks required in a tutoring session — listening, thinking, reading, speaking, writing — can be overwhelming. For example, when students are exploring ideas for a paper or talking through ways to organize them, the tasks of listening, thinking, and expressing thoughts clearly may be enough for them. It may be helpful for you to serve as scribe, jotting down key words or phrases *in the students' words.* At appropriate points, you can use these key phrases to help them get started writing or express themselves more clearly.

7. Plagiarism is not always the deliberate violation of rules that it seems. In our culture, we value originality in writing and regard a piece of writing as belonging to the person who produced it, so we cite the sources of borrowed ideas and words as we write, and we have rules about plagiarism. But not all cultures share our values. In some cultures, using the words of another is a form of flattery, and students may not understand that they need to document sources clearly. They may bring work written by a friend, following a cultural tradition that it is one's duty to help a friend or relative. Though you will need to explain our culture's rules and customs about citing sources and doing one's own work, be aware that ESL students may not be knowingly violating those rules.

Tutors tend to believe that they must be expert grammarians to work with ESL students, but that is not necessarily true. As Phyllis Brooks points out, "There is in the tradition of foreign languages and of English as a second language, a long tradition of the native informant: a sympathetic person who is literate and speaks well in his or her own language and can produce correct forms for students to imitate, or can suggest better forms for sentences than the student has tried, unsuccessfully, to produce" (48). Adults acquiring a new language rely heavily on imitation. You can help students rephrase a sentence and produce other sentences of the same kind. Producing such examples establishes patterns that students can begin to incorporate into their speaking and writing.

You also need to know that you will not be able to explain everything or answer all ESL students' questions about why some phrases or grammatical constructions work in certain ways. Eventually, however, you will become familiar with — and better able to help ESL students correct — some basic kinds of grammatical and syntactical errors.

The Writer with a Learning Disability

Some students have problems perceiving or processing information that interfere with their learning, but there is disagreement among experts about the causes and treatments of these problems. Only a trained professional can definitively diagnose a learning disability, for symptoms can best be described as clues; some are clear-cut, while others are more subtle. Even defining the term *learning disability* is difficult and controversial.

Students with learning disabilities may reverse letters, numbers, and even whole words, seeing or writing, for example, *was* for *saw.* They may confuse concepts like *up* and *down.* Their handwriting may be difficult to read, and they may misspell words in inconsistent ways. It is important to remember, however, that students with learning disabilities usually have average or above-average IQs.

Coping with a learning disability can be extremely difficult for students. I vividly recall one embarrassed and upset student who sat in my office, whispering as he explained that, unlike in high school, he had hoped to make it in college without special assistance. Could I please find him help with writing without making it too apparent to a tutor or letting his teacher know?

As a tutor, you need to be especially sensitive to the feelings of students like this. Without being condescending, make them feel comfortable about asking for and receiving help.

In many cases, students are aware of their disabilities and have learned to compensate. They know that they may need to take a test orally or with additional time, for example. They can often tell you how they learn best and what you can do to make your discussions and explanations most beneficial. If students tell you they have learning disabilities but do not offer information about their coping strategies, ask. Work with them as conscientiously as you would any student, but take additional care to involve the student, to structure and sequence material, and then to reinforce it.

Following are some strategies for working with students with learning disabilities.

1. Be patient; explain things clearly and repeat or rephrase if necessary.
2. Find a quiet place to work, one that minimizes distractions.
3. Teach to students' favored learning styles. The following section on learning styles contains specific suggestions to convey and

reinforce information to a variety of students. You might want to be creative and try combining approaches.

4. Be aware that a student with a learning disability may correct something and then immediately make the same error. Do not assume that he or she is lazy or has not been paying attention.

5. If students do not already compose on a word processor, encourage them to do so. Working on a computer avoids the need for recopying or retyping drafts, a process in which students may inadvertently introduce mistakes to otherwise correct material. In addition, the various programs available to check spelling can help students write with more confidence.

Learning Styles

Earlier you looked at the ways in which you and other tutors complete writing tasks. What you doubtless discovered is that each person has a different approach. The same is true of the ways in which we learn.

We tend to assume that others learn the way we do and are sometimes mystified when explanations or approaches that make perfect sense to us do not click with others. But not everyone absorbs and retains information in the same way, and different students respond to different tutoring strategies. If you have trouble getting through to a student with one technique — say, simply talking over a draft—you might want to try another approach, perhaps jotting down notes or drawing diagrams. As you become more familiar with your students and have a chance to try different approaches, you will gain a better sense of what they respond to best. Remember too that people retain more of what they learn when they are actively involved and engaged in the process.

Following are a few strategies that can be helpful.

VISUAL STRATEGIES

1. Rather than simply talking, work from written material, pointing to, circling, or otherwise highlighting information as you discuss it.

2. Make writing things down a part of the tutoring session by taking notes, jotting down examples, or drawing diagrams. When students leave, they will have something to take along — visual reminders of what you have discussed with them.

AUDITORY STRATEGIES

1. Read instructions, notes, or other material aloud, or have students read aloud.

2. Repeat or rephrase complicated directions.
3. Verbally reinforce points made in notes, diagrams, or other visual aids.

KINESTHETIC STRATEGIES

(*Kinesthetic* is based on the Greek word for movement.)

1. As you read through papers or discuss ideas, ask students to do the writing, underlining, highlighting, or diagramming.
2. Have students point to material as you talk about it.
3. Write sentences or sections of a paper on separate pieces of paper or file cards and ask students to rearrange them to find the most effective organization. (Self-stick removable notes are ideal for this activity.)

Student Concerns

If you have ever tried to write a paper after a fight with your boyfriend or girlfriend, when you are frantic about another course, or when living with your roommate has become impossible, you know that writing can be influenced by other factors in your life.

The following chart shows some common concerns of college students. As you look through it, think about the students who come to the writing center. Consider, too, that at various times, students may have additional anxieties. For example, freshmen or transfer students are adapting to a new school; many sophomores are choosing a major; seniors are facing job searches and increased independence; and returning students are coping with school, family, and job responsibilities. Though you cannot — and would not want to — be privy to all their concerns, it is good to remind yourself of the various personal issues that can affect students' writing.

Academic	Social	Lifestyle
Competition	Separation from family and friends	Independence
Classes (size, difficulty)	Roommates	Living arrangements
School size, bureaucracy	Friendships	Privacy
Parents' or personal expectations	Dating and relationships	Finances
Grades	Peer pressure	Job responsibilities
Study skills	Sexuality	
Test anxiety		

EXERCISE 5A

Think back over the students you have tutored and jot down some responses to the following questions.

—What concerns, besides those relating to their assignment, did they bring with them?
—How did they express those concerns?
—How did you respond?
—If you have not yet tutored, think about yourself over the past year. What personal concerns have you had, and how did they affect you as a writer?

CHAPTER 6

Computers and Tutoring

In the University of Maryland College Park Writing Center, a computer sits near the reception desk. Except on our busiest days, I usually find a tutor working at it. Generally, they are simply checking their e-mail, but sometimes it is Celeste, who has a daily Web assignment for an astronomy course; or David, who is seeking resources for his government paper; or J.B., who is updating our writing center homepage; or Gabrielle, who is putting together the next edition of our newsletter. These days, computers permeate our lives, and they also affect the ways in which we work with writers as we tutor them.

The writers we work with generally write on computers, and so we talk easily with them about manipulating text through cut and paste commands or about using features like spell check or a thesaurus. Some writing centers have computers available for writers and tutors to use while they confer, a factor that influences the tutoring techniques we use. The ability to move text quickly or highlight portions of it means that we sometimes employ particular strategies to make points clear. And because increasing numbers of writers have access to the World Wide Web, we often talk about using the Web to research topics and about how to evaluate and document the information students find there.

Some writing centers offer tutoring online. From a distance, a writer can send a paper through the computer, identifying questions or concerns about it. Later, the writer can retrieve the paper, complete with the tutor's written comments. In some cases tutor and writer can have a synchronous conversation in writing about the paper.

Computers affect us as tutors in other ways, too. We can access Web sites for OWLs (online writing labs) at numerous other writing centers to learn more about their services and, more important, to connect to their resources and to resources at still other sites. Through e-mail, we can join discussion groups devoted to tutoring and related topics.

This chapter does not attempt to list all the resources available online, but it does offer explanations of kinds of resources and important points to consider when you work with students or use these resources yourself.

Face-to-Face Tutoring at the Computer

In many ways, tutoring at the computer is similar to traditional face-to-face tutoring. You will still want to help student writers attend to higher-order concerns first, to prod them into thinking more by asking questions and mirroring what you hear them telling you about their paper. The advantage of tutoring at a computer is that it allows students to manipulate text easily. It also emphasizes the idea that writing is fluid and changeable rather than permanent. Ideally, tutoring techniques should take advantage of basic word processing functions and give writers strategies they can use after the tutoring session.

As a general rule, keep the writer in control of the computer and thus in control of the text. This positioning serves to remind the student writer (and sometimes, the tutor) that the writing is the student's. It also ensures that you serve as an audience, because two people cannot type simultaneously.

Several tasks that can be done with a pencil and paper can be done at the keyboard, often in more effective ways.

FREEWRITING

Freewriting at the computer can be a quick and convenient way to get started. Allow the writer time to type in a list of ideas or thoughts on a topic. As you and the writer talk about the list and relationships among ideas emerge, these thoughts can be rearranged on-screen using cut and paste commands. Occasionally people find it easier to freewrite on a screen that remains blank (often the case with those who have writer's block); you can adjust the monitor's brightness to accomplish this.

WORKING WITH A TEXT

To make writers more aware of their writing patterns, use the <u>underline</u> or **bold** commands. For example, ask writers who overuse forms of the verb "to be" to highlight all verbs in a portion of the text. You can then explain how to rephrase sentences or combine sentences to achieve more vigor and variety.

As you discuss the concept of offering support for ideas, have writers highlight the main idea or topic sentence in each paragraph. They can then see if each sentence in the remaining paragraphs supports that idea.

Using the return function, have writers break a portion of their text down into sentences. This allows them to concentrate on smaller units and see problems that sometimes get lost in standard text. In this way, you and the writer can look at matters of style (like sentence length and variety), of coherence (like transitions from one sentence to another), and of syntax (like fragments, comma splices, run-on sentences, and parallelism). The writer can also isolate whole paragraphs and then look specifically at the sentence order in each paragraph to consider rearranging.

Likewise, the writer can cut and paste the main idea (a key phrase) from each paragraph. After moving these key phrases to the end of the text, the writer can create a kind of outline of the paper. From here, you and the writer can consider such matters as thesis statements, organization, and coherence.

REVISING

The computer makes it easy to revise without erasing, scribbling out, or trying to fit new thoughts or ideas in squidgy places above and below the existing text. Using the return function, the writer can double or even triple space to gain room and insert comments, options, or definitions above or below the appropriate place in the text. Or the writer can insert a revised version of part of the text above or below the original to compare and choose. He or she can also leave large blank spaces in appropriate spots for further development of the text.

© 1985 Tribune Media Services, Inc. Reprinted by permission.

Conducting Research on the World Wide Web

The Internet is a networked collection of information stored in computers throughout the world, and a part of it — the World Wide Web (WWW or Web) — is a wonderfully useful tool for tutors. The Web allows for complex formatting of documents, which may contain text, images, sounds, movies, or a combination of these. Each document is designated by a unique URL (Uniform Resource Locator) that pro-

---

Useful Information about Domain Names

A domain name describes a computer's "location" on the Internet and allows you to ascertain what kind of organization or institution the file is coming from. Knowing how top-level domain names are registered can be useful as you conduct research on the Internet. This information can be important when you are trying to evaluate an electronic document. A domain name contains several components separated by a period or "dot." Reading a simple domain name

inform.umd.edu

from left to right (most specific to least specific), the first item (**inform**) is the name of the host computer (server), or hostname. The next item (**umd**) is the second-level domain name and is registered by an organization or entity with InterNIC Registration Services (http://www.internic.net). The last item (**edu**) is a top-level domain name. It describes the purpose of the organization or entity that owns the second-level name. A domain name may include other components between the hostname and the second-level domain name; these are called subdomains. In an e-mail address, the domain name follows the @ symbol and often consists only of a second domain and top-level domain name (**umd.edu**). Following is a list of some of the most frequently used domain names.

com	Commercial entities, that is, companies
edu	Registration limited to colleges and universities
net	Network providers
org	Miscellaneous top-level domain name for organizations that don't fit elsewhere (some nongovernment and non-profit organizations fit here)
gov	Agencies of the U.S. government.
int	Organizations established by international treaties or international databases
mil	U.S. military

---

vides location information. Following is a sample URL. The line below it "translates" the URL to show the kind of information the URL contains.

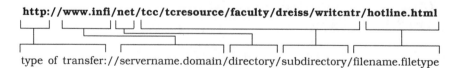

Authors create Web documents using a language called HTML (Hypertext Markup Language) that offers short codes to designate graphical elements and links. Links appear in the content area of a Web page. Lists may be one or more words highlighted by underlining, color, or both. They may also be images of icons with colored borders. Clicking on these links allows users to move easily between parts of documents and even between documents at different sites.

Evaluating World Wide Web Resources

Most print resources, such as journals and books, go through a review or filtering process, like editing or peer review. A draft of this book, for example, was read by several people who offered comments and suggestions for revision. Information on the Web, however, is largely unfiltered. In essence, the Web is a kind of vanity press; almost anyone can publish on it, and many resources are not verified by traditional publishers, editors, or reviewers. To help guide students conducting research on the Web — and as you conduct your own research — it is important to know criteria for evaluating the information found on the Web.

The three main elements of a Web document are its header, its body, and its footer.

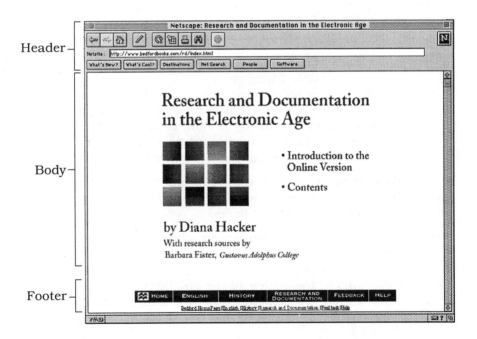

Header ⌐

Body ⌐

Footer ⌐

Research and Documentation
in the Electronic Age

• Introduction to the
  Online Version

• Contents

by Diana Hacker
With research sources by
Barbara Fister, *Gustavus Adolphus College*

By looking at these parts, you should be able to determine the following elements to use in evaluating the information contained in the document:

— Author or contact person (usually found in the footer)
— Institution, organization, or company (usually found in either the header or footer)
— Date of creation or last revision (usually found in the footer)
— Intended audience (determined by examining the body)
— Intended purpose of the document (determined by examining the body)
— Link to local home page (usually found in the header or footer)

Researchers need to consider the authority, accuracy, bias, and currency of any information — be it in print, on film, or online. What follows are some suggestions for determining these criteria when you or another writer looks at a Web resource.

AUTHORITY

With any material, you need to determine both the authors of the text and the basis of authority from which this author speaks. Because anyone can publish on the Web, it is sometimes difficult to determine authorship of a document, and frequently a person's qualifications for speaking on a topic are absent or questionable. If you do not recognize the author as well known and respected in the field, here are some possible ways you can determine authority:

— you found the address for or linked to the author's document from another, reliable, document
— the document gives substantive biographical information about the author so you can evaluate his or her credentials, or you can get this information by linking to another document
— the author is referenced or mentioned positively by another author or organization whose authority you trust

If the publisher or sponsor is an organization, you may generally assume that the document meets the standards and aims of the group. Some things to consider include:

— the suitability of the organization to address this topic
— whether this organization or agency is recognized and respected in the field
— the relationship of the author to the publisher or sponsor — does the document tell you something about the author's expertise or qualifications?

ACCURACY

You may be reading information presented by an author or organization unfamiliar to you and need to verify accuracy. Criteria for evaluating accuracy might include the following:

—other sources that the document relies on are linked or are included in a bibliography
—background information can be verified
—methodology is appropriate for the topic
—with a research project, data that was gathered includes explanations of research methods and interpretations
—the site is modified or updated regularly

BIAS

To determine bias, remember that any responsible author situates his or her work within a context. Since this context reveals what the author knows about the subject and what his or her stance on the topic is, check to see if

—the site was developed by a recognized academic institution, government agency, or national, international, or commercial organization with an established reputation in the subject area
—the author shows knowledge of theories, techniques, or schools of thought usually related to the topic
—the author shows knowledge of related sources and attributes them properly
—the author discusses the value and limitations of the approach if it is new
—the author acknowledges the fact that the subject itself or his or her treatment of it is controversial, if you know that to be the case

---

Backing Up for More Information

Working backward and removing sections of an URL, you can access other documents from the same site that may help you learn more about an author or document. Suppose you have questions about material in or the author of something you found at the following URL:

http://www.lsa.umich.edu/ecb/OWL/owl.html

http://servername.domain/directory/subdirectory/filename.filetype

With the URL displayed on the screen, delete the words representing "filename.filetype" (in this example, **owl.html**). Then go to the subdirectory (**OWL**) and see what is there. (You can then also delete the subdirectory in the same way to see what is contained in the directory **ecb**.) Sometimes, information in these other directories will enable you to better evaluate the author or material at hand.

CURRENCY

For many topics, currency is not an issue. Because the Civil War happened so long ago, for example, an older article on it may still be quite useful and valuable. For more contemporary topics, however, currency may be extremely important. You will need to consider whether the document:

—has a publication or "last updated" date or includes date of copyright
— gives dates showing when information was gathered
— gives information about new material where appropriate

Tutoring Online

Many writing centers have developed online tutoring sites, often to meet the needs of their student populations. As the number of nontraditional students on campuses increases, so too do nontraditional methods of learning and teaching. No longer do time and distance restrict learning to a classroom or a writing center, for students can attend classes from a distance using national cable television and satellite technologies. They can also access the writing center from a remote site, making tutorial assistance available to many students who might otherwise be unable to take advantage of it. From home, work, or computer lab, writers can send their papers to the writing center electronically. Generally, a tutor retrieves the paper, reads it, makes comments and suggestions for improvement, and then returns the paper electronically; some writing centers have technology that allows the tutor and writer to "chat" online about the paper, much as they would do face-to-face. Traditional student writers can benefit from such a service as well. For those who do homework at odd hours, live miles from campus, are temporarily laid up with a broken leg, or are simply shy, the online writing center solves some scheduling and distance problems.

Though some online writing labs offer a MOO, a text-based virtual environment that allows synchronous written conversation, for many tutors and writers, the biggest difference between online and face-to-face tutoring can be the time factor. With face-to-face tutoring, writers get immediate feedback. With online tutoring, however, they must often allow for a turnaround time that can range from a few hours to a couple of days, depending on the particular writing center and the way incoming papers are monitored.

Tutoring online has both advantages and disadvantages. Because the tutor and writer cannot see one another, the potential intrusion of some stereotypes diminishes. Gender and race are ambiguous with some names, and race and class often cannot be detected. On the other hand, tutors cannot use certain signals — like body language and tone of voice — to gauge the session's progress and make decisions about how to proceed. Occasionally, this may lead to confusion on the part of tutor or writer. Details that can be quickly straightened out in a face-to-face situation, like ambiguous language, sometimes confound either or both. When such confusion arises, the tutor and writer can simply ask clarifying questions if they are conferring through synchronous chat. Lacking chat capabilities, a tutor often e-mails brief questions to the writer before continuing with the paper. Likewise, writers can use e-mail to request clarification when they receive the tutor's responses.

Use of humor and sarcasm prove especially difficult online, and tutors must be especially careful not to offend inadvertently. Both tutors and writers report missing laughter, but they also say that as they work together over time, they come to feel like pen pals. With time, students grow accustomed to the back-and-forth nature of the tutoring online.

While lack of verbal exchange can be a disadvantage, some believe that writers gain from having a written copy of a tutor's suggestions. For ESL writers, in particular, a face-to-face session can be confusing if a tutor uses idioms or talks quickly; written comments can prove more understandable because the writer can read them over and over. On the other hand, written comments can also be perceived as more authoritative, permanent, and directive than intended. They can be printed and distributed to a wide audience. Therefore, you should document written answers to questions with authoritative citations whenever possible.

How does online tutoring work? Sessions begin just as face-to-face tutoring sessions usually do, with the writer telling the tutor about the assignment and the specific concerns he or she has about the paper. When students send papers electronically, they generally identify the course and the assignment, then explain what they would like the tutor to concentrate on as he or she reads. This use of electronic mail, however, changes the nature of the conference itself, slowing it down and focusing it on interpreting the student's text. In fact, some tutors report that online tutoring allows closer readings of student work. But just as in face-to-face tutoring, the tutor's ultimate focus should remain on helping the student to become a better writer rather than on simply making this particular piece of writing more effective.

Though online centers have different ways of assigning writers to tutors, generally tutors log on at regular intervals so that each paper is picked up in a timely manner. After retrieving the paper, the tutor must keep the writer informed. The tutor should e-mail the writer to say that he or she has received the paper and will be in touch soon. If a situation changes, the tutor should communicate with the writer: "I've been called out of town, but I've given your paper to Mary. You'll be hearing from her this afternoon." Reassurance is important. It should be conveyed in writing, not just by voice.

Here are some additional points to keep in mind when tutoring online:

1. Just as in face-to-face tutoring, establish rapport and make the writer feel comfortable. For instance, when you first work with a writer, introduce yourself and tell a little bit about yourself — your background, the length of time you have been tutoring, and the like.

2. Online writing centers ask tutors to append general comments about strengths and weaknesses at the beginning or end of a paper. In writing this overall statement, be encouraging and honest. Praise what is done well and explain why, but do not be too effusive. The writer can easily misinterpret "This is a great paper" to mean "I'll get an A." When you point out the paper's shortcomings, offer suggestions for improvement and/or explanations of rules.

   As you write comments, remember that length grants emphasis. Suppose a tutor writes, "Though content is thorough and organization effective, you need to look at your use of commas," and follows up with a page of rules and examples. Even though this comment addresses the more important aspects of the paper, the praise is short and even lies buried in a subordinate clause. Better to encourage by elaborating on what makes the content thorough and the organization effective, then talk about how misusing punctuation undercuts the writer's ethos and offer rules and examples.

3. Resist the tendency to simply edit. New online tutors report that because they work directly with a text, this tendency can be strong. Your purpose is not to proofread. In fact, simply editing does the writer a disservice, for he or she will not know what to do differently next time. Instead, point out recurring errors and explain the rules.

   Some online centers avoid this problem by limiting tutors' feedback to comments at the beginning or end of the paper. Others allow tutors to comment within the text by placing brackets or asterisks before and after their remarks to separate them from the student's text. As a way of modeling, some tutors edit a small portion of the text with explanations for each change and then suggest that the writer go through the rest of the paper and make similar corrections.

4. Watch your time. The length of a face-to-face session is determined by the clock, but that is not the case when you are tutoring with only a paper before you. If your online service has established time limits for each session, adhere to them. Should writers request or require more help than you can give in the allotted time, contact them to explain that fact and ask what they would like you to focus on.

Online Writing Labs (OWLs) and Other Electronic Resources

Many writing centers have established online writing labs, or OWLs, and more continue to do so as time goes on. Most of these OWLs give information about their services, staff, and location, and many offer access to worksheets, style manuals, and research tools. Many also take advantage of the Web's ability to link to documents at other sites, thus increasing the amount of available material.

One of the most popular OWLs is the Purdue University On-line Writing Lab, which you can find on the Web at

http://owl.english.purdue.edu

Many other OWLs link to Purdue's because it boasts an enormous data base. The Purdue OWL's stated primary goal is "to help writers improve their writing skills by offering them a variety of on-line services and materials and an introduction to searching for information on the Internet." It lists more than a hundred handouts, which can be searched by category, summary, or title. Writing-related resources include links to references, style and editing guides, business and technical writing, children and writing, professional organizations, ESL-related sites, and discussion groups. This OWL also provides links to reference materials in arts and literature, in science, engineering, and technology, in government information, and in social science as well as to more general references and indexes and search tools.

You can link to Purdue University's OWL, as well as other OWLs across the United States and Canada, through another useful and interesting Web site, the National Writing Centers Association, at

http://www2.colgate.edu/diw/NWCA.html

It offers information and links related to tutoring in several categories: writing center resources, writing centers online, resources for writers, tutor stories, e-mail discussion groups, and electronic print journals. The "Tutor Stories" section, which invites tutors to share their experiences, is particularly interesting on the Web.

Another type of online writing lab shifts the focus almost entirely from providing information to interacting with writers. Dialogue OWLs, like the University of Michigan's Online Writing and Learning Center **(http://www.lsa.umich.edu/ecb/OWL/owl.html)** and the University of Missouri's Online Writery **(http://www.missouri.edu/~writery/)**, invite writers from their campuses or from anywhere on the Internet to send in papers for critical response or to engage in conversations about writing. The Online Writery, for example, provides a tutoring list, an open discussion list, Web forums on topics writers wish to discuss, local newsgroups, and a MOO, which supports real-time interaction over the Internet. This OWL and others like it are based on the premise that writing is fundamentally conversation; thus engaging writers in written conversation is a productive and even enjoyable way to increase fluency and rhetorical skill. Though priority is given to their own students, these OWLs help to provide a community for isolated writers.

Electronic mail discussion lists offer a way for people with a common interest to communicate easily as a group. They provide a means of distributing a single message within minutes to everyone who subscribes. Lists allow subscribers to express their ideas ("I've just read Smith's article in *Writing Center Journal* and wonder. . . ."), to pose questions ("How do you handle uncooperative students who . . . ?"), to respond ("We've handled that problem by. . . ."), and to share information about meetings, conferences, and publications. By their nature, they also allow people to join quietly and simply listen, or "lurk" (and to leave unobtrusively as well).

Several groups discuss writing centers and writing-related issues. The site for the National Writing Centers Association contains a comprehensive list, but tutors may be interested in one of the following:

WCENTER (Writing center list)	**listproc@ttu.edu**
WCENTR-L (Moderated writing center list)	**listserv@mizzou1.missouri.edu**
WRIT-C (Writing center tutors and consultants list)	**listserv@tc.umn.edu**

To subscribe to one of these groups, send an e-mail message to the address listed. Leave the subject line blank. The message for the first list should read:

subscribe wcenter <your name>

Substitute the name of the list you wish to join for "wcenter" if you wish to join another. When you subscribe to a list, you usually receive a welcome message, which you should be sure to save. In addition to explaining the purpose of the list, it tells you how to *un*subscribe and how to get further help with using the list.

CHAPTER 7

Helping Everyone

Even if you are not an expert on the topic of a paper, you can still help the writer. I have often tutored students on subjects about which I had no knowledge, such as the benefits of shale for a geology paper and the treatment of knee injuries for a sports medicine paper. I have also helped students with literature papers about works I have never read. Regardless of a paper's topic, you can determine whether the ideas are presented in a cohesive and persuasive manner. You can look at larger issues like organization, style, and tone or at smaller issues like grammar and mechanics and determine whether the writing is effective. Still, it is helpful to know about conventions particular to certain assignments and to ask some specific questions.

If you are not familiar with the conventions of the kinds of papers discussed here, check your writing center resources — writing guides and handbooks, handouts, and other information that may be on file.

Lab Reports and Scientific Papers

A checklist for lab reports and scientific papers

1. Is the title short, and does it adequately describe the contents? For example, with the title "Substance Y Alters Blonial Structure of Elephant Bone Marrow," researchers interested in substance Y, blonial structures, elephants, or bone marrow should recognize that the article may be of interest to them.
2. Are the appropriate headings and subheadings included, in proper order? A typical scientific paper includes the following sections: title page, table of contents, abstract, introduction, body (with various subsections), conclusions, appendix. A typical lab report includes the following sections: title, abstract, introduction, methods, results, discussion, references.
3. Are the tone and style appropriate? Scientific writing, for the most part, is intended to be more factual than entertaining and is not embellished with descriptive language or anecdotes, humor, and dialogue.

4. Does the writer use passive voice, the generally accepted convention? The writer of a lab report, for example, should use the passive past tense: "Solution A was centrifuged," not "I centrifuged Solution A."
5. Are sentences short and to the point, expressing facts clearly and concisely? Does the writer answer all basic questions about the topic?
6. Have grammatical conventions, especially those relating to numbers, weight, and measurement, been observed?

Argument Papers

In argument papers, writers take stands on debatable issues, such as requiring comprehensive examinations for graduation, imposing curfews for teenagers, or abolishing capital punishment. The goal of such papers is to get readers to think differently about a certain issue or to persuade them to take a certain action. Writers of argument papers should envision skeptical audiences and build arguments that are strong enough to stand up to opponents' views. As they write, they anticipate readers' objections, refuting them or conceding points while indicating, for example, that there are more important issues to be considered.

A checklist for argument papers

1. Is the claim or proposition — what the writer is trying to prove — clearly stated?
2. Are all assertions supported by evidence?
3. Is the evidence — facts, interpretations of facts, opinions — appropriate? Data should be accurate, recent, and sufficient. Sources cited should be reliable.
4. Does the arrangement of evidence make sense? Does it emphasize the most important issues? Are there more effective ways of arranging the evidence?
5. Are facts, statistics, examples, anecdotes, and expert opinion placed properly? Are they used in the appropriate context?
6. Is the evidence carefully documented?
7. Is the reasoning sound?
8. Has the writer included any logical fallacies? (If you are unfamiliar with logical fallacies, refer to a writing textbook or handbook.)
9. Are terms that might be controversial or ambiguous adequately defined?
10. Have opposing arguments been considered and dealt with adequately?

Literature Papers

A literature paper analyzes, interprets, or evaluates a text, answering such questions as "What is the significance of the three scaffold scenes in *The Scarlet Letter?*" "What does the cherry orchard in Anton Chekhov's *The Cherry Orchard* represent?" "What is the significance of the setting in John Steinbeck's 'The Chrysanthemums'?" "How effective is the use of first-person narrative in John Updike's 'A & P'?" The writer of a literary essay should answer such questions with a meaningful and persuasive analysis that supports ideas and assertions with specific evidence from the text.

A checklist for literature papers

1. Does the writer use examples from the text to convincingly support his or her interpretation or analysis?
2. Has the writer avoided giving a simple plot summary?
3. Are parts of a work clearly and accurately referred to? Students need to indicate parts specifically, saying, for example, "the scene in which . . ." or "at the end of chapter 3."
4. Does the writer use the present tense when describing events in a work of literature, as is the convention? (This practice often confuses students. You might explain that the author is communicating to a present reader in the present time.)
5. Are titles properly punctuated or underlined? Titles of short stories, essays, and most poems appear in quotation marks; titles of books, plays, epics, or other long poems are underlined.
6. Has the writer referred to the author properly, using the full name initially and the last name in subsequent references?
7. Is quoted material properly punctuated, indented (if longer than four typed lines), and documented according to the format specified by the teacher?

Book, Film, and Play Reviews

A review describes and evaluates a book, film, or production of a play. Those published in newspapers and other periodicals help readers decide whether they wish to read a book or see a movie or play. They assume that readers are unfamiliar with the work and thus offer more summary than an analytical piece might. In reviewing a work, the writer often describes the criteria of evaluation and offers evidence (quotations, examples, and specific references) to support his or her opinions.

Though reviews cannot deal with every aspect of a work, they should focus on several. A play review, for example, might discuss acting, sets, costumes, lighting, and music, in addition to the play itself. A review commonly talks about the purpose, idea, or theme embodied in a work, often in relation to other similar works, and judges its quality by pointing out both strengths and weaknesses.

A checklist for book, film, and play reviews

1. Does the first paragraph include the title and other important information such as the author's or director's name?
2. Does the introduction give readers an idea of the nature and scope of the work? Does it establish criteria for evaluation?
3. Are evaluative terms or phrases, such as "good action" or "like a soap opera" defined? (What are the characteristics of "good action" or soap operas? How does the work embody those characteristics?)
4. Does an early paragraph briefly summarize the plot or contents?
5. Does the review make reasonable assertions and present convincing evidence (quotes, examples, and specific references) to support those assertions?
6. Is the tone appropriate? Does it suggest that the reviewer is being fair? Does it indicate respect for the readers?
7. Does the reviewer avoid overuse of phrases like "I think" and "in my opinion"? (Such qualifiers can weaken his or her assertions.)

Résumés

The résumé and cover letter are designed to get a job interview, not to secure a job, as some students believe. The résumé offers a prospective employer a quick look at an applicant's educational and work history and provides other pertinent information such as special skills, awards, and interests. It should be succinct and clear so that prospective employers can absorb information at a glance. (Keep in mind that the résumé you are working on may be one of hundreds that an employer has to read.)

While writing their résumés, students often downplay work experience that they think is irrelevant to the job they are seeking. They assume, for example, that being a bartender or a server in a restaurant has little or no relevance to a marketing position. What they don't realize is that the personnel manager of a marketing firm might be impressed by the fact that an applicant spent three years with the same restaurant, won the employee of the month award, or had responsibilities for handling money or training new employees. Students should consider how their experience might relate to a particular job and play up those relations in their résumés and cover letters.

A checklist for résumés

1. As it appears on the page, is the résumé pleasing to the eye? It should be balanced, not crowded at the top or off to one side.

2. Is all necessary information included? (Check for the student's name, address and telephone number, education, professional or related experience, and other experience.) References are not usually listed unless requested. Often, résumés include a line indicating that references will be furnished on request.
3. Is any unnecessary information included (such as birthday, height, weight, gender, number of children, political or religious affiliation)?
4. Are the parts logically and effectively arranged?
5. Is the length appropriate? Unless there's a good reason, a résumé should generally be no longer than one page, and certainly no longer than two pages.
6. If an objective is included, is it accurate? (As a professional or career objective, students sometimes write that they seek "an entry-level position as a . . . ," but an entry-level position is an immediate objective, not a long-term goal.)
7. Are education and work history (and other such information) in reverse chronological order, with most recent activities listed first?
8. Has the writer considered all relevant experience, such as volunteer work, internships, course work, and school projects?
9. Are job descriptions unnecessarily wordy? (For example, phrases like "responsible for" can often be omitted or tightened.)
10. In lists, are all the items in parallel grammatical form? (For example, in the list "writing proposals, trained new employees, planned staff meetings," "writing proposals" needs to be rephrased as "wrote proposals.")
11. Is the résumé error-free? Misspellings, grammatical mistakes, and other errors may cause employers to ask, "If this person is careless in writing a résumé, what kind of work can I expect from him or her?"

Cover Letters

Students should know that a résumé must always be accompanied by a cover letter. In these letters, applicants should clearly indicate the position they seek, mention how they learned about it (in a newspaper ad, through another person), and explain how their qualifications suit each requirement listed in the job description. Finally, they should request an interview.

A checklist for cover letters

1. Does the letter follow an acceptable format for a business letter? (See a handbook for a discussion of business formats.)
2. Is the letter addressed to a person rather than to a position? ("Dear Ms. Plotnic" is preferable to "Dear Personnel Manager.")
3. Is the position being applied for specifically identified at the outset?

4. Does the letter indicate how the student learned about the position?
5. Does the letter acknowledge all requirements mentioned in the ad or job description?
6. Does the applicant talk in terms of what he or she can do for the employer rather than the other way around? (With the exception of those applying for internships, which are set up to help students learn and gain hands-on experience, applicants are assumed to bring knowledge or expertise to a position; therefore, statements like "I expect to increase my knowledge about the accounting field" are out of place.)
7. Is the letter error-free?

Essays of Application

Students often ask for help with essays of application for undergraduate or graduate programs. Though you will need to consider the usual aspects of an essay — organization, tone, and grammar — you need to keep a number of other specific points in mind.

A checklist for essays of application

1. Does the writer establish early the point of the essay? Is the relevance of the information clearly established? Avoid the mistake made by one student, who wrote a lengthy essay describing her harrowing escape from her homeland. Though her point was that if she could withstand these rigors, she could manage medical school, she waited until the end to tell readers her reason for relating her story.
2. Does the introduction engage the reader? How will this essay fare against the many others that are being read? A note of caution: Readers want to see how an applicant differs from the other applicants, but they can quickly spot outrageous or excessive statements. The writer needs to consider the readers of the application: who they are and what they might be looking for.
3. On a related point, does the essay sound sincere and honest, or has the writer exaggerated? (For example, becoming a teacher to "change the world" is clearly beyond one person's capabilities.)
4. Has the writer completely answered the question posed? Some applications simply ask why one has chosen a particular career or program. Others ask applicants to discuss their strengths and weaknesses, ethics, work experience, accomplishments, or extracurricular activities.
5. Has the writer included sufficient evidence — often anecdotal — with details that show rather than tell? (For example, rather than saying "I am a caring person," the applicant should describe deeds he or she has done that demonstrate caring.)

6. Has the writer included extraneous details that don't contribute anything to the essay? (For example, Aunt Mary's illness may have led the student to consider becoming a doctor. Unless there is good reason, however, readers do not need to know what she prefers for breakfast or the kind of car she drives.)
7. Is the essay error-free? Misspellings, grammatical errors, and other mechanical problems may cause readers to question an applicant's attention to detail.

CHAPTER 8

Coping with Difficult Tutoring Situations

While tutoring, you will occasionally encounter some difficult situations. A student may come at the last minute, desperate for help. Or a student may come only at the insistence of a teacher and be difficult to work with. This chapter offers some specific guidelines for dealing with situations like these.

© 1980 United Features Syndicate, Inc. Reprinted by permission.

The Writer Who Comes at the Last Minute

You will sometimes encounter students who come for help just before their paper is due. Perhaps the paper is due in two hours and the student has only an incomplete draft with significant problems. Or the paper is due tomorrow morning and the student hasn't a clue as to what to write about. Such students may come to you in a guilty state of panic. How do you handle them?

DO

Help the student sort through his or her options and figure out what he or she can reasonably do in the time left. Be as kind and sympathetic as possible.

Help the student consider other options. If it is not possible for a student to complete an acceptable paper by the deadline, can he or she get an extension? Is there a penalty for turning in a late paper? If other options are not feasible, see what you can do to help the student in the time left.

DON'T

Scold or lecture the student about the need to write papers in a timely manner; you may mean well, but the student already knows what he or she has done wrong. Now he or she needs to think clearly and, with your help, figure out the best way to cope with the situation.

The Unresponsive Writer

Teachers sometimes require students to use the writing center, and occasionally such students bring with them an attitude of resistance. They may refuse to answer your questions, give halfhearted answers, or otherwise indicate that they do not wish to be there. Even their body language is often telling. They may slump in their seats, avoid eye contact, or avoid facing you. How do you help these students?

DO

Be patient and polite.

Remind the student that you are there to help and that the suggestions you offer are just that — suggestions that he or she may choose to follow or not.

Make sure the tutoring session is short but helpful. If you can improve one aspect of a resistant student's paper, he or she will see that coming to the writing center is not a waste of time.

Recognize that even your best efforts may not change students' attitudes, at least in the initial tutoring session. With hindsight, resistant students may realize that getting help with a paper is not altogether unpleasant. Another day, they may return of their own volition.

DON'T

Lecture students about your role or their unresponsiveness.

Lose your cool and become angry.

The Antagonistic Writer

© 1973 United Features Syndicate, Inc. Reprinted by permission.

For some students, writing a paper looms as an extremely frustrating—perhaps even impossible—task. They may be apprehensive about writing in general or upset about demands placed on them by a particular assignment or teacher. Often they view meeting these demands as beyond their control. If someone could only tell them exactly how to "fix" things, all would be well. Finding themselves in an impossible position, these students may become verbally aggressive, projecting their anger and frustration onto you, or they may show little interest in the suggestions you offer.

DO

Be patient, polite, and supportive.

Allow students to vent their feelings and tell you what is so upsetting.

Acknowledge students' anger and frustration with an *I* statement like "I hear how frustrated you are."

Using an *I* statement, rephrase what students are saying in order to help identify their emotions and problems. You might say, for example, "What I'm hearing is that you're frustrated because you can't figure out how to begin this paper."

If noises or other distractions are interfering with the session, try to move to a quieter place.

If students become verbally aggressive, politely tell them you are not willing to accept such behavior, but do so using an *I* statement. For example, you might say, "When you yell at me that way, I find it difficult (impossible) to listen."

Remind students that you are there to help and that the suggestions you offer are just that — suggestions that they may choose to follow or not.

DON'T

Lecture students about your role or their behavior.

Get into an argument or shouting match.

Become hostile or punitive with statements like "You can't talk to me like that!"

Look away and refuse to deal with the situation.

The Writer Who Selects an Inappropriate Topic or Uses Offensive Language

Occasionally, you may work with students whose papers are laced inappropriately with offensive language, such as racist or sexist terms. Or you may have difficulty helping with a paper that inappropriately takes an extreme and offensive position. What can you do in situations like these?

DO

Be patient and polite.

Remind students that they are writing for an academic community, and ask them to consider how their audience will react to the language or topic.

Respond as a reader and suggest, for example, "Some people might be disturbed by what you say here. I know I am."

Show students how to make language more acceptable. For example, you can explain options for avoiding sexist language and suggest alternative terms or ways of rephrasing. (Many handbooks and guides to writing include sections on avoiding and eliminating sexist language, and you might want to refer students to such discussions.)

DON'T

Get angry or hostile.

Take students' viewpoints or language personally.

Refuse to deal with the situation.

Occasionally, students may insist on their right to say what they wish and decline to make any changes. You might suggest to such students that they check with their teacher about the topic (or use of language) before continuing work on the paper.

EXERCISE 7A

Read through each of the following three scenarios twice. (If you are using this guide as part of a tutoring class, you and other tutors may want to act out the different parts.) As you go through the scenarios the first time, consider the following questions.

1. How is the tutor probably feeling? How do you know? What verbal and nonverbal clues indicate his or her feelings?
2. How is the student probably feeling? How do you know? What verbal and nonverbal clues can you find?

As you go through the scenarios the second time, consider the following questions.

1. What are the tutor's expectations?
2. What are the student's expectations?
3. What are some other ways the tutor might have handled the situation?

These scenarios provide excellent material for group discussion, and you can use the preceding questions as departure points.

Scenario 1

Tutor: Hi! [*Smiles.*] My name's Terry. We can just sit over here. Grab that chair. [*They sit.*] What can I do for you?

Student: Well, I'm Pat, and I have this paper [*hands it to tutor*], and, uh, my teacher said, I had to come here and, uh, get some help 'cause my last paper . . . [*looks down*] was a D.

Tutor: Then maybe we should just begin by reading through it. Do you want to read, or would you rather I did?

Student: [*Motions to tutor and mutters "You," then folds arms across chest and gazes off into space.*]

Tutor: [*Begins reading but is clearly having trouble. Stumbles over words and stops several times to clarify a word. As tutor reads, student occasionally sighs, taps fingers on desk and feet on floor.*] Listen, I'm really having trouble reading your handwriting. It would probably be easier if you read your paper to me. Would you mind?

Student: [*Hesitates.*] Naw, I guess not. [*Reads about halfway down page, suddenly stops and slams hand down on desk and looks at tutor.*] I really don't see the point of this.

Tutor: Well, it's just easier for me to tutor, to help you with your paper, if I hear what you've written.

Student: [*Waits a few moments, then tosses paper in front of tutor and speaks in a demanding way.*] Can't you just check it and fix it?

Tutor: When you come here and ask to have a paper proofread, the receptionist will tell you that the writing center isn't a proofreading service. It's a tutoring service. You can have a tutor look at your paper with you and discuss your problems and the tutor will try and show you how to correct them. We don't just correct students' papers!

Student: [*Annoyed.*] Well, I was told that you did! My friend said I could just have a tutor correct my grammar.

Tutor: [*Firmly.*] Well, I'm sorry. I don't tutor that way.

[*Silence.*]

Tutor: If you want me to continue reading through . . .

Student: [*Cuts tutor off, snatches paper away from tutor, looks quickly at watch.*] I just don't have time for this. Nothing against you, but I just don't have time for this. [*Collects papers quickly and gets up.*]

Tutor: [*Stares in disbelief.*] I'm really sorry. I just don't tutor that way.

Student: That's okay. It's nothing against you. [*Walks out.*]

Scenario 2

[*The tutor and student take seats at a table.*]

Tutor: Hi! I'm Pat. What can I do to help you?

Student: I don't know if you can. My teacher sent me here. And, well, I have this paper and I've sort of got a draft, well, at least a start of one I think, but I'm not really sure what to do. I wrote some stuff down anyway, but parts of it just don't sound right. [*Puts book and paper on table.*]

Tutor: What's your assignment?

Student: I have to write a book review for history. And there's no specific thing we have to write on — it's just, like a review. And the book's *Lincoln at Gettysburg*, you know, by what's his name [*reads name off book*], Garry Wills.

Tutor: [*Cheerfully.*] Great! Have you ever written a book review before? Do you know what you're supposed to include?

Student: Sort of. I think I'm supposed to give my opinion.

Tutor: Something like that. What you're supposed to do is evaluate the book and use evidence from the book — like quotes and examples and references — to back up what you say. So tell me some of your ideas. What did you like about the book?

Student: Well, I don't really know. [*Hesitates.*] It's, uh, you know. . . . What do you think about it?

Tutor: I don't know. I haven't read the book. But I can hear that you're a little confused. Why don't you just tell me some of your ideas, though, and we can talk about them.

Student: If you haven't read the book, I don't see how you can help me.

Tutor: Oh, but I can. In fact, it's probably better that I haven't read it. You'll have to explain things to me, and that'll help you sort out your ideas. If you just tell me what some of your ideas are, we can talk about them and I can help you think them through a bit. I do that all the time here.

Student: I just don't see how that will work. [*Frowns.*] I mean, if you haven't read the book . . .

Tutor: Yes, but *you* have, so it's really not a problem. I can tell that this is frustrating for you, but I *can* help.

Student: [*Hesitates.*] Well, uh, I, uh . . .

Tutor: You have read the book, haven't you?

Student: Oh, yeah. Well [*pause*], most of it. I mean, it's really long, and I don't know. . . . I can't get into it.

Tutor: Well, maybe you could tell me about the parts you have read, and we can at least start working from there. You said you wrote some things down. Tell me. . . .

Scenario 3

[*The tutor is sitting. The student sits down beside the tutor.*]

Tutor: [*Cheerfully.*] Hi! I'm Lee. What are you working on?

Student: I have to do a five-page paper analyzing this poem. It's due tomorrow morning — early. I don't know. It's really hard to do that stuff, don't you think? Why do teachers give assignments like this anyway?

Tutor: Well, they do. And I know, sometimes it's just not easy.

Student: [*Hesitates.*] Uh, I haven't really started it yet. Because I can't figure out what I'm supposed to do. Here's the poem and here's the assignment sheet. [*Hands poem and assignment sheet to tutor.*] What should I do? I really don't understand what the teacher wants.

Tutor: [*Glances at papers.*] Oh, I know that poem. [*Looks up.*] Did the teacher explain anything about the paper in class?

Student: Yeah, we're supposed to read the poem and analyze it, but I just don't know what she wants. [*Looks baffled.*] How do you analyze a poem?

Tutor: Well, let's see what the assignment sheet says.

Student: [*Sighs.*] I can't figure out the assignment sheet. It's so confusing to read. Can you read it and tell me what I'm supposed to do?

Tutor: [*Hesitates, glances at it, and then smiles.*] Sure, let me read it. It's short. [*Reads it over.*] Oh, here it is! At the bottom it tells you what to do.

Student: Oh, I didn't read that far. I got confused by the beginning stuff, with all those terms. The teacher never really explains anything to us. I hate that.

Tutor: Well, let's see if we can sort it out. The poem . . .

Student: [*Interrupts.*] Don't you just hate when teachers don't tell you what they want? If they just would tell me, I think I would be able to write it. [*Pauses and grins.*] So, you figured out the assignment? What am I supposed to do?

Tutor: [*Pauses.*] You know, what I'm hearing is that you're frustrated because you don't know what to do and the paper's due tomorrow. Let's look at the assignment sheet together. You can tell me which parts confuse you, and I can try and explain . . .

Student: [*Angrily.*] Look, I have to pass this class and I have to do the paper to pass it. Just tell me what to do! You know the poem and you know what I'm supposed to do . . .

Tutor: [*Firmly but politely.*] Yes, but I can't do the paper for you. I can help you, but it's your paper.

Student: I know, I know, I know, but what am I supposed to do? It's due tomorrow! [*Emphatically.*] I hate poetry!

Tutor: Well, I'm trying to help, but . . .

Student: Yeah, but it's so late. Just tell me what to say! Aren't you supposed to help me?

Tutor: I *can* help you, but if you don't want to do your share of the work, there's not much I can do.

Student: [*Grabs the papers.*] Yeah, well, thanks for nothing. I should have figured you tutors would be just like the teacher.

EXERCISE 7B

Think about a tutoring session in which you were not satisfied with the outcome. What made the situation so unpleasant, both for you and the student? How did you handle the situation? What are some other ways you might have handled it?

Outside Tutoring and Editing Jobs

Often individuals or companies contact writing centers looking for private tutors or editors. Following are some suggestions for dealing with prospective employers.

1. Negotiating pay

You are a professional who is being paid not only for the work you do but also for your experience, professional training, and level of education. Tutoring in a writing center gives you a certain amount of professional credence. Don't sell yourself short!

Pay is probably *not* the first matter you want to discuss — not because it is bad form, but because in order to discuss pay intelligently and fairly, you should know certain details about the job.

Questions about tutoring jobs:

— How much preparation time will be required (for planning, gathering materials, talking to instructors, and so on)?
— Are you responsible for planning the tutoring agenda, or will it be set by an outside source (teachers, SAT preparation books, and so on)?
— Will you be reading papers or reviewing exercises? (The former usually takes more time.)
— How often will you be meeting with the student?
— What is the student's skill level? Does he or she have any special problems?

Questions about editing jobs:

— What, precisely, does the employer expect you to do? Some people may say they simply need help "proofreading" when they actually want you to do major rewriting. You will need to determine if the job entails copyediting (tightening and clarifying sentences, fixing grammatical errors, and so on) or major revision (basically rewriting text into understandable English).
— How will the editing be done — by hand on a manuscript or on a computer disk?
— Is typing the manuscript (as well as editing it) involved?

—Will you be expected to use your own computer, paper, or other supplies?

—How much freedom will you be given? Can you edit on your own or will you have to work closely with the writer?

To help determine what to charge, talk to other tutors who also tutor or edit. What do their jobs entail with respect to the details listed here, and how much do they charge?

Whether tutoring or editing, arrange to be paid at *regular* and *frequent* intervals (for example, after each tutoring session). Do not allow charges to accumulate. Keep a record of the payment schedule. Show the person paying you that you are keeping the record up to date by taking it out each time you are paid and noting the payment.

2. Negotiating time

➤ *For tutoring:* In tutoring situations, keep track of time, and try not to go over the limit; if you do, people will tend to expect that you will work longer for them regularly. You cannot expect people to pay for your preparation time, so factor this time into the per-hour rate you agree on. Also, people do not usually pay for travel time, so take this time into account also.

➤ *For editing:* Keep meticulous track of time. The clock should be running from the moment you pick up the work until the time you put it down for the day.

3. Arranging meeting space

If you are tutoring someone, you might want to suggest a public library or study room on campus. Public study places, rather than someone's home, are often more conducive to getting work done. They tend to offer fewer distractions for the person being tutored, and they also provide you with greater control over the environment.

4. Planning for the long term

➤ *For tutoring:* Will you be expected to work toward certain goals (such as helping a student pass an exam)? How much time do you have to meet those goals, and how much responsibility do you have for their successful completion?

➤ *For editing:* Will you be expected to work toward certain deadlines? What are they? Will there be rush periods?

Tutors Ask . . .

The following questions were posed by tutors. See what kinds of suggestions you can come up with for dealing with the situations they describe. If possible, share your ideas with other tutors. (You may use the questions as departure points for group discussion.)

1. What can I do to make students do more of the work in a tutoring session? How can I help them get more of the answers themselves?

2. What can I do with papers that seem just fine? I worked with someone the other day, and I just couldn't come up with any real suggestions for improving the paper.

3. The other day, I had a student who was working hard, but she kept talking about how she thought the assignment was too difficult. I tried to sympathize, but I was afraid she'd think that I agreed with her. What could I have done?

4. What can I do if I don't fully understand the assignment? A student tried to explain his assignment to me so I could help him get started, but he was so vague, and I couldn't really tell what the teacher was looking for.

5. What should I do when a lazy student comes into the writing center assuming that the tutor will come up with all the ideas? I tried so hard to get this particular student to think and come up with his own ideas, but he just sat there silently or said, "I don't know."

6. What can I do for students who come in ten or fifteen minutes before closing and can't come back the next day? Should I try to help them anyway? How?

7. Should I allow students to walk out of the writing center with glaring errors still in their papers? What impression will teachers — or even those students — have of the writing center when that happens?

8. In a session yesterday, I worked with a student who was quite frustrated with her schoolwork, her assignments, and her professor. What made me most uncomfortable was her attitude toward the professor and his assignments. She seemed to be quite negative from the start. I could feel the tension. Her stance and facial

expression indicated that she was feeling a great deal of stress. I got her to calm down a bit, and I basically let her get out some of the gripes that she had. After letting off some steam, she seemed to feel a bit more relaxed and comfortable. What else can I do to help in this kind of situation? Is it worthwhile to have a tutoring session?

9. Some students just want a quick fix and get impatient when I start explaining. How can I get a student to really listen when I explain why something is wrong?

10. Sometimes a student leaves with an attitude that suggests that I was of no help whatsoever. When this happens, how much should I blame myself? The student? What can I do to avoid this kind of problem?

Tutors Talk: Judging What They Say

In each of the following examples, indicate what the tutor said or did that was or was not effective and explain why. Describe what the tutor might have said or done instead. (You may use the examples as departure points for group discussion.)

1. Wow! You have a problem with run-on sentences. Let me get you a worksheet that explains how to fix them and an exercise to practice with. When you finish, let me know and I'll correct it.
2. Hi, I'm Eric. Let's sit down over here. You can put your book bag there and then tell me what you're working on.
3. Help you now? We usually take people on the hour. I've just tutored two people and I'm tired. Besides, I have an econ exam this afternoon, and I was hoping to get a few minutes to review stuff. How much help do you need?
4. Here in your paper, you say that "most upper-level courses require research papers." If you really want to convince your audience, you need to support that statement with an example or two. Can you give me one — a specific one?
5. This paper is great! Your teacher's sure to love it. I had Dr. Brown last semester, and he likes anything about World War II.
6. I always get confused between restrictive clauses and nonrestrictive clauses. I don't want to tell you the wrong thing, so let me get a grammar handbook, and let's check out the rules.
7. You keep saying "I think . . . ," but your teacher already knows that you're writing this paper and that the ideas are yours. Let's take this sentence. How can you rephrase it without using "I think"?
8. Your paper's due tomorrow and these notes are all you have? You should have written at least a draft by now.
9. You have a lot of misspellings and grammar problems. Let me read you this paragraph and show you what happens to me, as a reader, when I have to deal with so many mistakes.
10. You're arguing for abortion? I don't think I can work with you. I'm against it.

11. It doesn't really matter if English is your second language. You have to fit in — you know, "When in Rome, do as the Romans do."

12. Do I ever sympathize! I used to make this same sort of mistake all the time. Then I learned what conjunctive adverbs are and how they work with semicolons and commas. Let's take this sentence where you use the word *however,* and I'll explain.

13. Why don't I just read your paper, and then I'll tell you what I think.

14. I'm not sure what your point is in this paragraph. Why don't you just tell me what it is you're trying to say?

15. I'm so glad you got me for a tutor. I took that class last semester and I have lots of ideas about that poem.

16. Let me play devil's advocate. You're arguing against fraternities, but I belong to one and there are lots of advantages.

17. You do have a problem if this paper's due this afternoon. Let's see what we can do.

18. I'm really just here to help. Anything I tell you is just a suggestion. You can take my advice if you want, but you don't have to.

19. This looks like a really hard assignment. I don't quite understand it either. Professor Cunningham never does explain things very clearly. What do you think you're supposed to do?

20. Look, all you have to do to make this better is put in some more details. Here, when you look out of the window of the plane, talk about how tiny everything is. And with the food, say it tasted bland or delicious or whatever, then when you get to the landing part, say it was bumpy, smooth, loud, quiet, whatever it was. You'll have a good paper then.

Annotated Bibliography

PERIODICALS

The following periodicals provide articles on issues and trends of interest to writing centers and tutors.

The Writing Center Journal (a publication of the National Writing Centers Association, an NCTE assembly). Published twice a year. SUBSCRIPTIONS: Dave Healy, Editor, University of Minnesota, General College, 140 Appleby Hall, Minneapolis, MN 55455-0434. E-mail address: healy001@maroon.tc.umn.edu

Writing Lab Newsletter (a publication of the National Writing Centers Association, an NCTE assembly). Published in ten monthly issues (September–June). SUBSCRIPTIONS: Muriel Harris, English, Purdue University, 1356 Heavilon, West Lafayette, IN 47907-1356. E-mail address: harrism@omni.cc.purdue.edu

BOOKS AND ARTICLES

The following bibliography lists some of the books and articles that writing center directors and tutors have found informative and useful in their work with students. The list is by no means comprehensive, but it should serve as a good starting point for investigating and learning more about the writing process and tutoring.

The Writing Process

Elbow, Peter. *Writing without Teachers.* New York: Oxford UP, 1975.
   Elbow describes a process approach to writing, moving from freewriting through drafts that allow the text to "grow" as writers interact with other writers or consider their own expectations or the demands of literary genres.

Flower, Linda S., and John R. Hayes. "A Cognitive Theory Process of Writing." *College Composition and Communication* 32 (1981): 365–87.
   The authors discuss the structure of the composing process by analyzing writers' descriptions of the choices they make while writing.

_____. "Problem-Solving Strategies and the Writing Process." *College English* 39 (1977): 449–61.
The authors offer a heuristic of planning, generating ideas in words, and constructing for an audience. The heuristic encourages analytical and experimental attitudes toward writing.

Harris, Muriel. "Composing Behaviors of One- and Multi-Draft Writers." *College English* 51 (1989): 174–190.
This article describes differences between the composing behaviors of writers who write one draft and those who write more than one and discusses implications for tutoring and teaching both kinds of writers.

Leki, Ilona. *Understanding ESL Writers: A Guide for Teachers.* Portsmouth, N.H.: Boynton/Cook, 1992.
This book offers insights into the writing behaviors and errors commonly made by ESL students as well as ways to respond effectively to their writing.

Murray, Donald M. "Write before Writing." *College Composition and Communication* 29 (1978): 375–82.
Murray identifies and discusses exigencies that help the writer move toward a completed draft.

Perl, Sondra. "A Look at Basic Writers in the Process of Composing." *Basic Writing: Essays for Teachers, Researchers, and Administrators.* Ed. Lawrence N. Kasden and Daniel R. Hoeber. Urbana: NCTE, 1980. 13–32.
This essay focuses on the writing process used by some basic writers and the differences between this process and that of more skilled writers.

_____. "Understanding Composing." *College Composition and Communication* 31 (1980): 363–69. (Also included in *The Writing Teacher's Sourcebook.* 3rd ed. Ed. Gary Tate and Edward P. J. Corbett. New York: Oxford UP, 1994. 149–54.)
Looking at the recursive nature of writing, Perl suggests that good writers return to key words or phrases in a text to recover and attend to a "felt sense" of what they wanted to say.

Rose, Mike. *Writer's Block: The Cognitive Dimension.* Carbondale: Southern Illinois UP, 1984.
Rose looks at case studies to discover differences between writers who block frequently and those who seldom block. He suggests that no one approach to teaching writing should be considered applicable to all situations.

Shaughnessy, Mina. "Diving In: An Introduction to Basic Writing." *College Composition and Communication* 27 (1976): 234–39. (Also included in *The Writing Teacher's Sourcebook.* 3rd ed.

Ed. Gary Tate and Edward P. J. Corbett. New York: Oxford UP, 1994. 321–26.)
Shaughnessy looks at how teachers change in response to working with basic writing students.

_____. *Errors and Expectations.* New York: Oxford UP, 1979.

Sommers, Nancy. "Revision Strategies of Student Writers and Experienced Adult Writers." *College Composition and Communication* 31 (1980): 378–88
Sommers analyzes the differences between what students and experienced writers do when they revise.

Strunk, William, Jr., and E. B. White. *The Elements of Style.* 3rd ed. New York: Macmillan, 1979.
This book succinctly discusses rules of usage, principles of composition, matters of form, and commonly misused words and expressions; and it offers advice for achieving a satisfactory style.

Wall, Susan V. "The Languages of the Text: What Even Good Students Need to Know about Re-Writing." *Journal of Advanced Composition* 7.1–2 (1987): 31–40.
Wall discusses revision as an opportunity for invention and a means for coming to terms with conflicting ideas.

Williams, Joseph M. "The Phenomenology of Error." *College Composition and Communication* 32 (1981): 152–68.
Williams encourages instructors to reconsider harsh attitudes toward errors in student writing, noting that even teachers often overlook errors in their own and others' writing and speech.

_____. *Style: Ten Lessons in Clarity and Grace.* 5th ed. New York: Longman, 1997.
Williams offers clear and concise advice and exercises for writing clearly, simply, and elegantly.

Zinsser, William. *On Writing Well: An Informal Guide to Writing Nonfiction.* 5th ed. New York: HarperCollins, 1994.

Tutoring Writing

Amigone, Grace Ritz. "Writing Lab Tutors: Hidden Messages That Matter." *The Writing Center Journal* 2.2 (1982): 24–29.
Amigone examines the importance of nonverbal cues and messages in tutoring.

Branscomb, Eric. "Types of Conferences and the Composing Process." *The Writing Center Journal* 7 (1986): 27–35.
Branscomb identifies types of conferences (those dealing with process, content, or skills) and discusses them in relation to the writing process.

Brooks, Phyllis. "Peer Tutoring and the ESL Student." *Improving Writing Skills: New Directions for College Learning Assistance.* Ed. Thom Hawkins and Phyllis Brooks. San Francisco: Jossey-Bass, 1981. 45–52.
Brooks examines ways in which peer tutors can help ESL students become more competent writers.

Edwards, Marcia H. "Expect the Unexpected: A Foreign Student in the Writing Center." *Teaching English in the Two-Year College* 9.2 (1983): 151–56.
Edwards examines differences between foreign students and American students and how these differences affect the tutoring session.

Harris, Muriel. "The Roles a Tutor Plays: Effective Tutoring Techniques." *English Journal* 69.9 (1980): 62–65.
Harris discusses the effective tutor as a coach, commentator, and counselor.

————. *Teaching One-to-One: The Writing Conference.* Urbana: NCTE, 1986.
This book offers a rationale for conferences, a discussion of conference goals, tasks and activities, and suggestions for diagnosing problems and teaching skills.

————, and Katherine E. Rowan. "Explaining Grammatical Concepts." *Journal of Basic Writing* 8.2 (1989): 21–41.
This study examines students' difficulties with learning grammatical concepts and suggests effective strategies for overcoming these difficulties.

Hynds, Susan. "Perspectives on Perspectives in the Writing Center Conference." *Focuses* 2.2 (1989): 77–89.
Hynds examines how dissonance between tutor and student expectations can be resolved, and she uses case studies to explore interpersonal dimensions of tutoring.

Konstant, Shoshana Beth. "Multi-Sensory Tutoring for Multi-Sensory Learners." *Writing Lab Newsletter* 16.9–10 (1992): 6–8.
Konstant suggests ways of teaching students with learning disabilities by appealing to their strongest perceptual channels.

Morrow, Diane Stelzer. "Tutoring Writing: Healing or What?" *College Composition and Communication* 42 (1991): 218–29.
Making analogies to her medical training and experience, Morrow describes her tutoring experiences and concludes that a model of mutual participation, where tutor joins student in the search for answers, is best.

Mullin, Joan A., and Ray Wallace, eds. *Intersections: Theory-Practice in the Writing Center.* Urbana, Ill.: NCTE, 1994.
Essays in this collection explore a variety of theoretical strands in writing center work.

Murphy, Christina, and Joe Law, eds. *Landmark Essays on Writing Centers.* Davis, Calif.: Hermagoras, 1995.
This collection of essays that have shaped and informed writing center work is divided into sections on history, theory, and practice.

Murphy, Christina, Joe Law, and Steve Sherwood. *Writing Centers: An Annotated Bibliography.* Westport, Conn.: Greenwood, 1996.
This comprehensive resource covers scholarship on writing center theory and practice.

Murray, Donald M. "The Listening Eye: Reflections on the Writing Conference." *College English* 41 (1979): 13–18.
Murray describes and analyzes his experiences with student-centered conferences.

North, Stephen M. "The Idea of a Writing Center." *College English* 46 (1984): 433–46.
North looks at the perceptions teachers often have about writing centers and proposes that centers attempt to produce better writers primarily by talking to writers about writing.

Reigstad, Tom. "The Writing Conference: An Ethnographic Model for Discovering Patterns of Student-Teacher Interaction." *The Writing Center Journal* 2.1 (1982): 9–20.
Reigstad identifies and explains three conferencing models: teacher centered, collaborative, and student centered.

Stay, Byron, Christina Murphy, and Eric H. Hobson, eds. *Writing Center Perspectives.* Emmitsburg, Md.: NWCA Press, 1995.
These eighteen selected papers from the First National Writing Centers Conference in 1994 cover a range of theoretical and practical approaches.